The Awakening

Lessons From My Journey of Finding True Identity in Christ

Amanda Stout

ISBN
E-book: 979-8-9948758-0-3
Paperback: 979-8-9948758-1-0
Hardcover: 979-8-9948758-2-7

Library of Congress Control Number: 2026903732

Connect with the author at her website: https://ariseinfaith.app/

Dedication

This book is firstly dedicated to my Lord and Savior, Jesus Christ, without whom nothing in this book would be true or real. I owe my life and my story to Him.

Secondly, this book is dedicated to my husband Paul who has unwaveringly supported me in all me endeavors, especially this one. I am so grateful for his partnership.

Finally, this book is dedicated to all who resonate with it. To all who read this work and feel seen, heard, validated, and understood. You have been voiceless for far too long, but not anymore. Not on my watch.

Contents

INTRODUCTION

There is a lot of conversation happening around identity in the world today. It's common to be asked "how do you identify" about just about everything, but around gender and sexual orientation especially. One glance at the world and we can see that there is an epidemic of people who are seeking to belong and from that desire, they are rooting their identity in everything *except* that which will actually fulfill them in the long run.

But don't make the mistake of thinking that this is just found in the secular world, it's rampant in the church as well. Christian men, women, and youth alike are choosing to root their identity in things that are unstable and fleeting.

Work. Money.
Family. Relationships. Sex.
Power. Fame.
Independence.
Sports. Movies. Shows. Music.
Educational, Medical, Health, or other personal choices.
Roles or positions in the Church or other volunteering/ charity involvement.
What denomination or theological/doctrinal position they do or don't affiliate with.
The list could go on and on.

Even in the church, cliques and groups form around these and other things people choose to base their identity in. And then we wonder why the Church is so fragmented, why identity crises run rampant in the culture, and why mental health issues are on the rise. It's because we have misplaced our identities - which is another way of saying that we are practicing idolatry.

We try to find purpose, meaning, and belonging in everything but the one thing that can fully fill that need: God. Ultimately this is idolatry because an idol is not just some statue people worship, an idol is anything or anyone that we go to first or desire more than or otherwise place above God in our lives. Even good things like relationships, work, ministry, or hobbies can become idols if they replace God in our attention, affection, and devotion.

This is a human problem that has existed since the Fall. The first sin was one revolving around identity - both God's and ours. The enemy whispered lies and planted doubt about God's character and identity into Adam and Eve's ears, and they believed it. The enemy caused them to wonder, "is God really good? Does He really want my best? Is He holding out on me?" and that doubt gave room for the enemy to then plant lies about Adam and Eve's identity, leading them to desire and take the forbidden fruit. And it's the same today. Identity is at the core of most, if not all, sin. When we are solid in our identity in Christ, we are empowered to resist temptation. But like Peter walking on the water, we falter when our eyes are not fixed on Him. The enemy has used the same core tactics since the beginning: he tries to malign the character and identity of God in our eyes, creating a divide between us and our Creator that allows him to then destroy, erode, or shift our identity.

In the following pages that is what we are going to explore. We are going to discover why identity is under such attack, expose the tactics of the enemy, expose lies we believe about God and ourselves, learn the Truth, and take some really practical steps to shift from believing those lies into believing the Truth.

Through these pages you'll find pieces of my personal story sprinkled in. This is not meant to be some great theological or scholarly work. This is simply me sharing pieces of my own journey and the revelations that the Lord has given me along the way. I've learned that the root cause of much of the pain in our lives is found in a misplaced identity. I know because I've lived it. The battle for my identity started waging early in my life, with the enemy pulling out most of his tactics. I was under assault on all fronts, but God. God came in when I was just two years old, granting me a saving knowledge of Him that kept me hungry and open to Him.

That doesn't mean things got better. Quite the contrary. I experienced a significant amount of abuse growing up in my childhood home, much of it deeply impacting my identity. I believed many of the lies I am going to expose and break down in this book, and that resulted in me growing up thinking that there was something deeply wrong with me. I believed the lie that I was broken, that the way that I am naturally wired is fundamentally flawed. I thought that I had to be something other than who I actually am in order to be acceptable to people and God. I spent YEARS of my life suppressing my true self, trying to fit the mold I was being pushed into, at least enough to be accepted. But it was never good enough, and I ended up stressed to the max, broken, anxious, depressed, self harming, even suicidal at my lowest point. Through it all I kept crying out, asking the Lord what was wrong with me, what do I need to do to fix myself and stop all the pain and hurt. Then one day the Lord broke through with His truth in a way that I was finally able to hear it, and it started me on a path that has completely changed how I live my life.

People who knew me before I received my healing would say that I've changed, that I'm a different person. And in one sense they are right, but a more accurate way to describe it is to say that I've become who I've always been all along, who God made me to be. I'm embracing and stepping into the identity He intended for me all along. Note the present tense there. I'm not perfect and I haven't arrived - it's still a daily journey of making the choice to operate from my God-given identity, replacing the lies the enemy tries to whisper with God's truth. But that is the beauty of free will and the journey of faith. It's our choice to walk this path, and as we do so the Lord blesses us and heals us.

As you read this book you may be confronted with some uncomfortable truths. Your theology and belief system may be challenged. You may find yourself feeling uncomfortable and frustrated, or possibly validated and seen. This book is meant to bring up and bring to light things we in the church like to ignore and dismiss. If that's hard, it's ok. Let it be hard, and process through it anyway.

In certain portions of this book you will find application exercises, reflection questions, and prayer scripts. I strongly encourage you not to skip over these but to work through them deeply and genuinely, especially in any sections where you felt challenged or convicted.

Before you move forward with reading the rest of the book, please take a minute to pray and invite the Lord to be with you and speak to you as you read. Ask Him for wisdom, clarity, and discernment. Ask Him to highlight what it is that He wants you to learn and take away from this book. Invite Him to convict you where needed, encourage you where needed, and to work in your heart as you read and process the information found in this book. Ask Him to bind any attempt of the enemy to twist and distort your understanding, instead ask for your eyes to be opened to God's truth - even if that means challenging things you've believed your whole life.

Are you ready to begin your journey? Let's dig in and expose the enemy's lies, learn God's truth, and make the shift to walking in the fullness of our true identity.

PART ONE

IDENTITY AND WHY THE ENEMY WANTS TO DESTROY IT

Identity: the distinguishing character or personality of an individual.
(The Merriam Webster Dictionary)

Identity. It's the core of our being. It is our sense of self, and the sense of where we fit in the world. It's also one of the first and main things the enemy attacks and tries to destroy, erode, or shift - whatever he can do to weaken us - because it is from our identity that we make choices and live our lives. A solid and biblically accurate sense of our identity enables us to live victorious over his schemes, while a tainted sense of identity makes us more susceptible to the lies and machinations (schemes) of the enemy, and less effective for the Kingdom of Heaven.

But there is an even deeper, more personal reason why the enemy seeks to destroy our identity.

While every human being has their own unique identity and personality, they all share one key core piece: every human being is born with the identity of being made in the image of God. This is something not even the heavenly beings can claim - it is a unique gift to humankind. We hold a special place in the order of creation because of this fact, and the enemy is incredibly jealous of us.

He was created the archangel of light, chief worshipper of God, and protective covering over God's Throne (Ezekiel 28:12-19). But that wasn't enough for him. He aspired to become God. He tried to define his identity on his own terms, and was cast out of heaven for it, thereby losing the identity he did have (Isaiah 14:12-15). He then had to watch while we humans were given what he wanted - we were created in the very image of God.

God also infused us with free will and the ability to be creative as He is creative. No other creation, including angelic and heavenly beings, has this ability. They can only imitate or twist what is already created. The ability to be creative is totally and completely unique to humankind. This is part of what makes us a reflection of God, and the enemy hates this about us just as he hates God. But we can't walk in the fullness of our potential if we don't know or believe it, so our identity becomes one of the first things the enemy will try to attack and undermine from the moment we are conceived, usually in the form of trauma and planting lies.

So the first thing that must be understood when learning about and embracing our identity is that we are in a battle. All day every day, war rages around us. It is not always something we can see, because it is happening in the spiritual realm, but it is there nonetheless, and it directly impacts you. Likewise, you directly impact it, whether you realize it or not.

Part of this very real battle is happening over you - your soul, your purpose, your destiny, and your identity. The Lord and the enemy are fighting over you. If the enemy can undermine your sense of self, he has an upper hand in the battle. The younger he can get to us to distort our identity, the better for him and his designs. And while he is not omniscient (all-knowing) like God, he is smart, he is crafty, he can see in the spirit the tendencies and the giftings God has bestowed on us, and he can sense our God-given calling and destiny to a degree. Using that information, the enemy attacks our identity where we are the most gifted in an attempt to reduce our threat to his kingdom and designs.

So from conception, he is studying you and throwing attacks your way. Everyone is hit differently due to the variables of personality, family relationships, socioeconomic status, etc, but everyone will face an attack on their identity at some point in their life, typically at least once before the age of 8, and many times after.

There's a strategic reason for that. By the age of 8 or so, a person's core belief system is pretty much set. Our brains are neuro-plastic (able to adapt and shift and change connections) and therefore we are able to shift our belief systems any time we want, but it is a much harder and longer process after age 8. That is why children are under such attack in our society right now. If the enemy can get to them young, he is more likely to succeed in reducing their impact for the Kingdom of God. And the bigger the calling, the bigger the attack. So if you feel like you've been slammed on all sides relentlessly, take heart! It means you have the potential to be a huge threat to the enemy, and you are in good company.

While it might be daunting or even scary to think about the cosmic battle that is raging around you and the fact that both sides have a plan for you, there is massively good news: you have free will. This means that your destiny is in your hands - YOU get to decide which path you are taking. However, a word of caution: there is no neutral. You're either in or you're out for either plan. If you choose neutral you default to the enemy's plan. In fact, he LOVES it when you choose neutral. Satan loves nothing more than a bunch of lukewarm, neutral "Christians". He can arguably do the most damage with such people because they know enough of the Bible to be self-righteous and proud and judgmental, but not enough to be filled with Holy Spirit fire such that they genuinely reflect Christ - or they've suppressed it. It is through them that he is often able to undermine the work of the Holy Spirit in some, and deeply hurt or even destroy others.

The enemy often works through certain people to try and destroy the identity of those around them. But here's the amazing thing about your identity - it's yours. No one can take it, change it, or reshape it without your permission. Identity is rooted within us. Now we can choose to base our identity on things outside of ourselves, but that's our choice. As Eleanor Roosevelt once said "No one can make you feel inferior without your consent." We can choose to let what someone else thinks or says dictate who we believe we are, but it's still our choice. Which also means that regardless of how or when we may have given power over our identity to others, at any given time we can take it back and/or adjust it. How amazing and empowering is that?

On top of that, we can educate ourselves so that we are aware of the tactics of the enemy and are able to recognize when he is coming after us. We also are able to fight back, resisting him so that eventually he will flee from us (James 4:7).

Are you ready to uncover his schemes so he can no longer deceive you and hold you captive?

Let's go.

Reflection Questions:

How do you feel about the idea of there being a cosmic battle over your soul?

Have you allowed the thoughts and opinions of others to shape your sense of identity? If so, who?

Has their influence left you feeling empowered and in a healthy place with the Lord, or has it created a wedge between you and God and left you feeling empty, heavy, or full of shame, guilt, and fear?

Are you willing to do the work to reclaim your true identity?

PART TWO

THE TACTICS THE ENEMY USES TO ERODE AND DESTROY OUR IDENTITY

The enemy has a myriad of tactics he will use to erode, steal, kill, and destroy our identity, and with it our destiny. However they can be broken down into two categories or strategies:

1. Twist and distort how we see and think of God
2. Twist and distort how we see and think of ourselves.

The very first tactic the enemy ever used was to undermine how humans see God. It started in the Garden of Eden. He started his assault on identity by questioning and planting seeds of doubt about God's character, integrity, intentions, and relationship to Adam and Eve - in other words, he planted seeds of doubt about God's identity. Adam and Eve took the bait, questioned God's character, disobeyed God, and therefore opened the portal that allowed sin and death to enter the world. From there, it changed how Adam and Eve saw themselves. After eating the fruit (choosing to believe and act on the lie) they became aware of their nakedness and felt ashamed. It is the same today. That slippery snake comes in whispering questions and lies about who God is and when we take the bait, he latches on and destroys us.

Strategy One: Twist and Distort How We See God

In order to align our identity correctly, we have to start by making sure we are clear on the identity and character of God. Because if we don't know or trust Him, how can we stand strong in the identity He has given us? Because we are made in His image, an inaccurate view of Him will automatically translate into error in how we view ourselves. And the enemy knows this. That is why he focuses so much energy on twisting and distorting our perception of God from an early age. One of the most pervasive tactics he uses is to plant lies about who God is.

Common Lies About God that We Believe

Regardless of the religion, denomination, or overall background we were raised in, we all have some sort of idea about who God is.

Some people believe He's the big old guy in the sky just waiting to zap us if we step out of line.

Others believe He is "love" - accepting and affirming everyone and everything, with a "just do you boo" attitude.

Others believe that He is a myth, a fairy tale, a story we tell ourselves to make life more bearable.

Still others believe He exists but is uninterested in our individual lives.

The list could go on and on with ideas people hold about God - some accurate, others warped by poor teaching or just straight up wrong.

The following exploration is not an exhaustive list of incorrect beliefs we can hold about God, they are simply the ones I personally have overcome, as well as some of the most common ones I see when working with clients. However, I've found that many of the different incorrect beliefs about God that we hold can be boiled down into some version of the following beliefs. As you read through them, I strongly encourage you to pray and ask the Lord to show you where you have an inaccurate understanding of His character, heart, and identity. Then, as He shows you things, take the time to process it with Him so that you can correct any place where you are seeing Him incorrectly.

Common Distortion of God's Character 1: God is like ____ authority figure (parent, teacher, pastor, etc.)

What has always been so interesting to me is that one of the most common tactics the enemy uses is to use the dysfunction of our parents (or other authority figures) to distort our view of God. He will use our parent's imperfections to plant seeds of doubt, mistrust, and confusion about the character, nature, and identity of God. This is honestly such a cheap shot on Satan's end because of what an easy target it is. Our parents are the first example of authority we experience in our lives, and due to that association, our perception of God is so often shaped by our relationship with our parents and how we view them. This means that even if we have a relatively good cognitive (brain/head) understanding of who God is, it doesn't always translate accurately into our daily lives and hearts.

For some people, this tactic to use our parents to suggest lies about God can be more effective than others. For people who were raised by relatively healthy parents who consistently chose to pursue the Lord and grow and heal that which was unhealthy in themselves, the negative interactions are typically outweighed by the positive ones, and while there may be some beliefs about God that need adjusting, overall such people come out of their childhood home and experience relatively unscathed.

For others, like myself, who were raised by unhealthy

and even abusive parents, this tactic often gives the enemy the results he's looking for. An unhealthy, abusive parent can be a huge stumbling block for a person to understand the true character of God because we tend to project the character of our parents onto God. After all, one of the most common descriptors used of God in the church is that He is a good Father. But for those of us who did not have good fathers, that metaphor actually hinders intimacy with the Lord. We naturally tend to project the characteristics, good and bad, of our parents onto God.

As we grow older, the list of authority figures in our lives expands, and even if the enemy can't get to us through our parents, he will try the same general tactic with other authority figures. Using this subconscious projection of wounds from authority figures onto God is another flavor of this tactic the enemy uses, regardless of who the authority figure is. It can be parents, but it can also be teachers, extended relatives, pastors, even government officials and civic leaders. It can even be an older sibling or peer that we look up to. The enemy loves to use the unhealthy places in others to wound us and undermine our sense of identity so deeply that we blame that wound on God. From those wounds come wrong beliefs and lies that we believe about God.

Different wounds can create different beliefs. For example, emotionally absent authority figures suggest that God is distant and doesn't care about us as individuals. Overly authoritarian authority figures and fire-and-brimstone teaching suggest that God is angry, judgmental, and just can't wait to punish us. Conditional love from humans suggests that God requires us to earn His love and acceptance. A lack of healthy boundaries in our key relationships can either suggest that God doesn't actually care what we do and is just an impotent, permissive entity, or that He is a selfish being who will push His agenda onto us regardless of what we want. Since God is the ultimate authority, we tend to naturally assume God rules with the same characteristics of the authority figures we meet in our childhood.

<u>*Reflection Questions:*</u>
What were your parents like? What kind of people were they?

What was your relationship with them like?

How did you interact with them?

How did they interact with you?

How did you feel around them?

How did you feel about them?

What do you believe they thought of you?

Do you see any ways in which those interactions, feelings, beliefs, and expectations around your parents may be similar to how you interact, feel about, believe, and expect God to show up?

The issue of projecting the character of our authority figures onto God gets muddied even further when those authority figures behave that way in the name of the Lord, and pull out various Scriptures to support why what they are doing is ok. This leads to a web of incorrect beliefs about Him and His character. Let's explore some of them.

The Three Most Common Incorrect Beliefs About God Created Formed by Our Experience of Authority Figures

1. God is angry, judgmental, and can't wait to punish me

Many of us were raised in harsh, controlling, and even abusive environments. Whether it was at home, church, school, our neighborhood, or a combination of factors, the overall atmosphere was one of authority figures exercising absolute authority and maintaining their rule using fear, intimidation, and manipulation. For them, rules and image, not relationship, is the name of the game. They have rules, standards, and expectations and you will fall into line with them or else experience the consequences - which are harsh and often abusive.

This was my experience. My parents, the churches we went to, the overall attitude of the homeschool support group we were members of, and the college where I got my B.A. all had the same, very specific box of what being a "good Christian" looked like, and if/when I didn't fit the mold I was punished, shamed, and spiritually and emotionally (and occasionally physically) abused. Their words said one thing, but their behavior told me that what I looked and behaved like on the outside mattered far more to them than the state of my heart. Even worse, every correction came with Scriptures (usually out of context or twisted) to support their point which only further strengthened my incorrect beliefs about God's character and identity.

One of the most significant of these incorrect beliefs was that God is angry, harsh, judgmental, and just waiting and watching, looking for any reason He can find to punish me. But honestly, for me it went further than that. Deep down it felt like He enjoyed punishing me, that it was fun for Him to nitpick, micromanage, and then zap me. That anything positive I did was ignored, but the minute I made a mistake, WHAM! Punishment. Subconsciously, I projected how my parents dealt with me onto God.

Of course I could never admit that though, because the Bible says God is love and that behavior is not loving. So I was stuck in this limbo of cognitive dissonance[1]. My experience of authority figures taught me that punishment and fear is the way that God rules, but His word says He's loving and gracious and merciful. But then the words and the actions of the authority figures in my life often didn't line up (and often crossed the line into gaslighting[2]), so I wondered if maybe that's what God is like too (it's not). But deep down I knew that the Bible's description of God HAD to be the right one, I just needed a better understanding of and evidence for His true character.

I gained this understanding and evidence in a couple of ways. First, I threw away all my commentaries and human perspectives and interpretations of the Bible and I really, truly, dug into my Bible with fresh eyes. I released everything I thought I knew and I explored what HIS word says about His character. Then I held anything humans had to say as well as what my experience suggested to be truth up to the Truth of Scripture, kept what lined up and discarded what didn't. Then I started making choices in line with that Truth. I stopped listening to those who taught something different. I sought the Lord and asked Him to start giving me evidence of good, Godly authority to replace the evidence of the abusive, toxic authority I experienced growing up. And as the good, loving, and faithful God that He is, He did.

---

[1] A strong sense of mental discomfort, overwhelm, and stress that results from holding two conflicting beliefs, values, or attitudes, OR when your actions do not line up with your beliefs.

[2] The psychological practice of manipulating someone into questioning their own sanity, memory, or powers of reasoning.

Reflection Questions:
Has your experience led you to believe that God is angry, judgmental, and harsh?

Are there specific memories, examples, or conversations/ teachings that stand out for you as key moments when this belief was created or deepened?

Are you willing to put aside that belief and the supporting experiences in order to open yourself up to seeing and experiencing something different from the Lord? Are you willing to open yourself up to the possibility that He is different - it's the human beings who represented Him to you that are angry, judgmental, and harsh?

2. God's love is conditional and I have to earn His acceptance

Another incorrect belief we can pick up from how authority figures relate to us is that God's love and acceptance is conditional and we have to earn His favor, love, and blessing. We develop this belief because we were raised in environments where we had to earn anything and everything that was considered a privilege or luxury by those who were in charge. For some of us, this even extended to basic necessities like affection, education, food, and rest - literally nothing was provided to us until those in authority felt like we had "earned" them.

For me personally, this incorrect belief about the nature of

God has been one of the biggest roadblocks I've had to face in my journey to a healthy relationship with the Lord. From a young age my experience told me that nothing in life is free, everything comes with a cost. I had to earn my right to eat and be educated by working and completing an exhaustive list of chores - and I'm not talking about normal chores and expectations like making your bed and putting away your laundry. I'm talking Cinderella "clean the whole house before you can go to the ball but then when you're done I'm adding five more things" level here. The list was so heavy as I grew older I often didn't have time for school work until after dinner (we were homeschooled, so that's how my parents got away with that). I had to earn the acceptance of my parents, many of my "friends", and church by checking their boxes. By the time I was in my mid teens I was expected to pay for my own necessities like toiletries and clothing (and sometimes food), despite not having any sort of regular income. Rest and fun were things that I had to do extra work to earn the privilege of experiencing.

So I know first hand how hard it is to really accept and walk in the unconditional love of the Lord. For a long time whenever He blessed me, I would wait and watch for the catch - the part where I had to pay for the privilege or blessing He bestowed. But it never came because there wasn't one. Patiently and consistently, the Lord worked on my heart and provided me with the experiences and safety I needed to understand and accept that this idea of having to earn everything is the opposite of His heart.

I now know and truly believe that there is nothing I need to do to earn His love, salvation, or relationship with Him. It's all freely given, with an invitation to be healed and whole and empowered with a kingdom purpose and identity to boot. All I have to do is be willing to believe, receive, and embrace what He wants to give me. All I need to do is be willing to be transformed and obey His directions, and then He does the heavy lifting.

This isn't to say once we accept our identity in Christ we sit around doing nothing; part of our kingdom purpose is to work WITH Him to further the kingdom. BUT His burden and yoke (work) for us is easy, light, and joyful when we walk aligned with Him, and His love for us is not based on what or how much we do. We do not have to earn His acceptance; we do not have to work to be saved. If we are genuine Christ-followers, there is literally nothing we can do to lose His love and grace and acceptance. If this is an area where you are struggling, keep reading. We will be discussing how to break free from all of these lies later on in this book.

Reflection Questions:
Has your experience led you to believe that God's love is conditional?

Are there specific memories, examples, or conversations/ teachings that stand out for you as key moments when this belief was created or deepened?

Are you willing to put aside that belief and the supporting experiences in order to open yourself up to seeing and experiencing something different from the Lord? Are you willing to open yourself up to the possibility that He is different - it's the human beings who represented Him to you that withheld love and acceptance based on their perception of your behavior?

3. God is capricious, unsafe, unpredictable, and even enjoys messing with me - basically, He is a narcissist[3].

Then we've got the authority figures who were unpredictable, emotionally unstable, and made us feel like we needed to tiptoe and walk on eggshells around them. Some of them may have been genuinely unwell with real mental health disorders needing better support (which is still no excuse for toxic behavior, but does impact how we address that behavior). However, the ones I'm talking about were/are simply toxic, unhealthy, possibly narcissistic, people who were willing to utilize any means necessary to maintain the sense of control they desired. The unpredictability of their moods and demands kept us in a state of hyper-vigilance, wrecking our adrenals and nervous system. On some level, these figures might even enjoy the mental and emotional havoc they wreak on us because this state of high stress means we are unable to think clearly enough to find a way to push back and escape their control.

They would pull out a variety of emotional abuse tactics - love bombing followed by emotional evisceration, gaslighting, guilt, shame, various other forms of manipulation, straight up lying, and expecting us to be mind-readers and cater to their every whim - just to name a few. Their goal is to create a specific "perfect" image as well as be the person who is in control and on top. They thrive on keeping those around them in a state of emotional instability, entirely focused on and dependent on them and their whims. Experiencing this type of abuse - for that is what it is - especially at a young age, can create so many wrong perceptions of what God is like and who He is.

The expectation of experiencing this hot and cold, unstable, unpredictable behavior combined with unrealistic expectations from our authority figures often gets projected onto God, creating beliefs that cause us to emotionally distance ourselves from Him. Some of these beliefs are that God isn't

---

[3] a personality disorder characterized by an exaggerated sense of self-importance, a need for admiration, and a lack of empathy for other people

trustworthy or safe, or maybe that God actually won't tell us what we need to know, nor will He teach us. Another one is that He expects us to just know what to do, how to do it, and to do it right the first time, and if we mess up He will punish us. Overall, these beliefs work together to develop the core belief that God is unpredictable, unstable, even capricious[4] like the pagan gods of old.

Often we experience the inner turmoil of cognitive dissonance between what we read and hear about God and what we expect from Him because that's what we've learned to expect from authority figures. Can you see the mental torment that happens? Do you recognize it? Have you experienced it? Even if it's not conscious, those of us who have developed these beliefs deep down experience this tension and torment, longing for a relationship with God, yet fearing it at the same time.

This also was my experience in the home, church, and overall atmosphere that I grew up in. I was raised by parents who exhibited all of the previously listed behaviors and more, and I spent the first 24 years of my life in church and educational environments that not only allowed but actively taught, approved of, and exhibited those behaviors as well - all in the name of "Christian Living". Which is beyond ironic because anyone who has a real relationship with Christ can tell you that these behaviors are the opposite of what Christ modeled for us. It takes a massive twisting and misinterpreting of Scripture to make it support the positions these types of leaders take, but most of them are absolutely masters at using the Bible to support their abuse.

This combo of emotional and spiritual abuse is one of the most challenging forms of abuse to heal from because it leaves invisible scars on both your soul and your spirit that take much longer to heal than a physical wound. As anyone who has experienced these things can tell you, it often breaks something inside your brain. Prolonged exposure to this behavior leads

---

[4] given to sudden and unaccountable changes of mood or behavior

you to start believing that you are crazy, broken, and the problem. These types of people are so good at making themselves appear so amazing to those outside the inner circle that no one believes you when you try to tell them what things are like behind closed doors. This makes it so hard to get help, and only furthers the fears that you are crazy or the one in the wrong.

This was my experience. The dysfunction of my parents and other authority figures in my life created deep wounds that impacted how I saw both God and myself. While in my head I knew that God is not like the authority figures who hurt me, my heart struggled to trust Him. The wounds from these people got transferred and projected onto God on a subconscious level. On top of that, these wounds also fed lies about myself that I believed, creating a vicious cycle of hopelessness and despair.

Maybe that's where you are. Maybe your experience of authority figures has told you that God is cruel, capricious, and conditional. Maybe that's even how your Church presents Him. Or maybe your theology teaches something different, but deep down you struggle to trust Him because you have been so deeply hurt by people who claim His name. Maybe you want to feel intimate and connected and close to Him, but you're scared because in the past intimacy only led to pain. Maybe you have been or even are currently in a similar environment to what I have described. If that is you, please hear me: you are NOT crazy, and you are NOT the problem. There are people who will believe you and help you, some of whom are listed in the resource list at the end of this book. Please, look them up, pick the one that resonates with you, and reach out to them. If you know you need healing but you're struggling to reach out for it, read on. There is hope and healing for you.

Reflection Questions:
Has your experience led you to believe that God is unstable and narcissistic?

Are there specific people, memories, examples, or conversations/teachings that stand out for you as key moments when this belief was created or deepened? What are they?

Are you willing to put aside that belief and the supporting experiences in order to open yourself up to seeing and experiencing something different from the Lord? Are you willing to open yourself up to the possibility that He is different - it's the human beings who represented Him to you that are unstable and narcissistic?

Have you found yourself longing for closeness with God, yet fearing it at the same time? If so, what specifically are you afraid of? Be as detailed and honest as possible when you journal this out.

Common Distortion of God's Character 2: God is not truly good - otherwise known as the problem of pain and suffering.

While using authority figures to taint our view of God is one of the most prevalent of the enemy's tactics, another one is to use circumstances around us to cause us to question God's goodness, kindness, love, power, authority, and more. Loss, injury, accidents, betrayal, suffering, and the general consequences of evil in the world touch all of us at some point in our lives. Some experience it earlier, some later, some experience it more frequently, but no one is immune from experiencing intense pain at some point in their life.

These moments of pain bring their own crises of belief. It is natural to wonder how and why a "good" God would let such horrific things happen, especially to people He says He loves. It doesn't feel loving to let someone suffer so deeply. In those moments of wrestling and grief, the enemy wastes no time in coming in to whisper doubts about God's character into our hearts. The details shift, but the core doubt that he tries to feed us is "If God loves/cares/etc, why did He let ____ happen?" or "If God loves/cares/etc, He would do ____". Often it is hard to find an answer that actually feels convincing, and unfortunately certain bad theology that is rampant in the church only makes the issue worse.

Bad Theology

Incorrect theology of suffering and pithy platitudes can sound lovely and on the surface seem to give a purpose to the pain. But underneath, it often is unsatisfying, and those who are suffering are left not only in pain, but with their faith shaken even further. Well meaning comments like "God wants us to suffer well", "God's ways are higher than our ways", and "At least it wasn't ____" only end up feeding the doubts and sense of abandonment we face when dealing with suffering.

While God does allow, use, and redeem the suffering we go through, He is not the author of it and He does not enjoy watching us suffer. An unhealthy understanding of the balance between God's sovereignty and human free will can create some really damaging approaches to suffering. On one hand, if we believe that God is in total control and completely sovereign, the suffering must be in His will and we humans, worms that we are, have no right to question His ways, means, and purposes. We must simply bear our lot in life without complaining - in fact we are required to be grateful and welcome suffering. While there are Scriptures that talk about being joyful in trials and persecutions and exhort us to see them as a testing and proving of our faith, to say that our suffering is God's will and that we are not to question it is an imbalanced, inaccurate understanding of God's sovereignty. This perspective on suffering also tends to skip over the key element that allows us to have the joy these Scriptures refer to in suffering - a genuine, intimate, connected personal relationship with God.

This incorrect theology is rampant in the church, but is completely wrong and is actually just a Christianized version of the type of pagan Greek Philosophy of Fatalism that was taught by Plato. Fatalism says that everything is in the hands of destiny or chance or fate (or in this case, God), and that there is nothing one can do about it except grin and bear one's lot in life, for there is no fighting or escaping Fate. One of the things that I personally find so frustrating about this error in theology is that it begs the question: if God really is good, wouldn't He use His sovereignty to protect us from pain? If He has total control, why wouldn't He use that control to protect His people? Christian Fatalism does not have a good answer to these questions, and it therefore feeds doubt and lies about the goodness of God and/or encourages people to disconnect their brain and thought life from their faith life. It promotes a form of Christianity that discourages questioning and thinking for oneself. Those who question this theology are accused of lacking faith and trust in God - a straw-man tactic that allows the theologians who promote it to avoid the accountability of actually having to support their position or do real research into the origins of it.

On the other hand, if we believe that the free will of

humankind runs the show, then the natural conclusion when faced with pain and suffering is that my suffering is somehow my own fault - or at least something I can control. Some will go so far as to say that a deficiency in our faith or choices is what causes our suffering (which is the same straw-man argument Christian Fatalists use). And while of course there is a type of suffering that is entirely our fault - the consequences of our own sin and choices - there are many types of suffering that we have little to no say in such as illness, accidents, or the choices of others. Additionally, no one really would choose suffering yet it happens, so that does beg the question of do we really have free will and control over our own lives? Just as Christian Fatalism is an imbalanced take on the Biblical concept of God's sovereignty, so too is this over-emphasis on free will an imbalanced perspective of the Biblical truth of human free will. The universe is not so black and white, and accurate understanding comes when we find ourselves more in the middle of these two concepts.

The Balance Between God's Sovereignty and Human Free Will

God is sovereign AND humans have free will. God created the universe with a certain set of laws and rules, both natural and supernatural. One of those laws is that humans have free will to decide how they are going to live their lives. We have the freedom to choose our thoughts, our object(s) of worship, and many other things throughout our lives. Because we all have this free will, sometimes we (or others) sin, and there are natural consequences to that sin that at times may harm others, not just ourselves. Or we are hurt by others' sin through no fault of our own. God cannot necessarily stop the sin or always remove the consequences of the sin because that would violate our free will. God abides by His own laws and rules, so He won't violate our free will. Otherwise He wouldn't be good and perfect and just, and we wouldn't actually have free will.

God’s sovereignty does not mean complete control, nor does it mean that God’s will is always what happens. God’s will is that none should perish (2 Peter 3:9), but some still do by their own choice. This clearly shows that the things that happen in the world are not always in line with God’s will. There is a difference between sovereignty and imposing one’s will. God is sovereign and will ultimately win, but not by becoming a dictator.

The best human illustration I can think of for a balanced idea of God’s sovereignty is that He knows all the possible outcomes and variables, and makes the best choices accordingly, like a master chess player. When playing chess you cannot control what moves your opponent makes; you can only observe, analyze, and if you are very good at the game, think multiple steps ahead, taking into account multiple variables. Then you make your moves accordingly, and win. That’s what God does. He is outside of time, as well as being omnipresent (everywhere all at once all the time), omnipotent (all powerful), and omniscient (able to see and hear everything including the thoughts and intentions of all beings). Being outside of time, He can see the end from the beginning and He can see all the variables and possibilities. Based on those variables and possibilities, He makes His moves. This is how nothing surprises Him and he can orchestrate everything to work out “for the good of those who love Him, who are called according to His purpose” (Romans 8:28) as well as for His glory without violating free will.

So while God cannot always stop hard, bad, painful things from happening, what He can and does do is redeem it when it is given to Him. So we can take the pain, hurt, suffering, abuse, etc that we have gone through - whether it’s our own fault or not - and give it to Him and He will redeem it and turn it into something beautiful. He doesn't desire for anyone to perish, nor does He delight in the pain of His people, but because He is a good and just God, He follows His own laws and respects our autonomy as beings with free will who can choose to obey or not. So it's not His will that you suffered, but He promises to redeem that suffering and turn it into a blessing if you are willing to (and then actually do) give it to Him.

As we've seen, bad theology around the balance between free will and God's sovereignty has made the issue of pain and suffering confusing and a place that gives the enemy a lot of room to plant doubt about who God is. On top of that, because humans tend to be so uncomfortable with pain, and the church as a whole has not been very emotionally intelligent and trauma aware, when we go through hard things we are typically encouraged to gloss over or even skip the process of grieving and experiencing of the pain and jump straight into the spiritualizing of our experience. This results in many of us stuffing our emotions, feeling shame for even having them, and gives room for bitterness to take root in our soul.

<u>Reflection Questions:</u>
Have you believed or been taught one of the extremes - Christian Fatalism or Exclusive Free Will?

Have you been hurt by one or both of these approaches to pain and suffering? If so, how?

How did that impact your view of God?

Crises of Faith

Seasons of suffering can get even harder when you have a close relationship with God and hear His voice and the things that happen seem to be the opposite of what you thought you heard. This is one of the things I had to wrestle through when my third child, Faith Anne Elizabeth, died in 2022. When she was diagnosed with a Congenital Diaphragmatic Hernia (CDH) at her 20 week anatomy scan, it was devastating. I spent the rest of her pregnancy praying for healing. The Lord told me there would be healing and confirmed it through others. I stood on that, agreeing with what I thought the Lord had said. Then she died at 26 days old after a valiant fight to overcome the complications of CDH.

What a crisis of faith. How do you trust God when He promised something and it doesn't look like it happened? I struggled with this for months after her death, until my personal life coach at the time reminded me that God wants me to be real. He doesn't want me to just come to Him with my best, He wants me to come with everything - even the raw and the real and the messy. So I did.

I told Him how betrayed I felt. I asked Him why He told me He would heal my daughter if He wasn't really going to. I was real and raw and open with Him. To my surprise, He didn't smite me or even correct me. He simply met me there, put His arm around me and cried with me. Then, when all my tears were spent, He told me that He did heal her, just not the way I was expecting. She's not gone, she's with Him. That this wasn't a simple thing, there is no simple explanation for why things turned out this way. There were so many variables and pieces and things that I can't understand yet, but I didn't mishear Him, I just selected the part I wanted to hear and interpreted it to be what I wanted it to mean. Because if I'm honest, I knew deep down the whole time that her only real healing was going to be in heaven.

Then He showed me a part of how He was using her short life for my good and His glory. He showed me how her death led to my oldest child accepting Christ, and how the grief and pain I was experiencing was softening my heart and revealing other, deeper, areas I needed healing. Then He gave me a glimpse of the future and how Faith receiving her healing in heaven instead of on earth would ripple out to impact so many more people. He promised healing - I interpreted it to mean that Faith would be healed on earth. What He meant is that He would heal her in His arms, and then use the brevity of her life to heal me, my family that is still here on earth, and by extension all the people we are called to minister to.

Through this experience with the Lord, I learned a couple things. Firstly, that when He says He wants us to come to Him with everything, He means it. He's not going to get mad at us for coming to Him with our fears, doubts, anger, and hurt. In fact, He wants us to. And when we do, He meets us with compassion, understanding, and healing. The Psalms are a perfect Biblical example for this principle. They are full of lament, questions, and pain. But they also show the process of how when we take that lament, questioning, and pain to God, He will help us carry it and give us comfort.

Secondly, I experientially learned how when I take everything to God and give it to Him, He redeems it. The Scriptures talk about how God promises to exchange our ashes for beauty, our mourning for joy, our heavy burdens for a light yoke. While I had cognitively known and believed that, it was in this season that I experientially learned it. I went to Him with my pain, anger, fear, and doubt, and He took it and gave me in its stead comfort, peace, and purpose.

The best part is God does not play favorites. He will do the same thing for you. I know you're scared. I know that being real with your emotions was used against you your whole life and you are afraid that the Lord will punish you if you were honest about how you feel with Him. But He won't. He knows anyway and He wants you to give it to Him - but He won't rip it out of your hands. You have to willingly give it to Him so He can transform it and relieve the burden you've been carrying.

Reflection Questions

Have you experienced a crisis of faith in your life? Has there been a time when you thought God promised something but it didn't happen like you expected and it shook your faith?

What happened?

Are you willing to open up and ask God to give you His perspective on it? (Note, God's voice is never shaming, condemning, or hopeless. If the voice your hearing sounds like that, it's the enemy)

Religious Abuse

Another common tactic the enemy will use to plant lies in our soul about God are incorrect teaching about and representations of God in church or other religious settings. We've already covered a lot of the unhealthy behaviors and subsequent lies they can plant in us in the previous sections on authority, but one thing we haven't discussed yet is how those environments treat those who question the establishment, and how that can further isolate and damage one's relationship with God.

In religiously abusive environments like those described in the previous sections, victims are guilted and shamed into silence. Genuine study of the Bible and exploring other viewpoints than the accepted narrative is heavily discouraged, even punished. Those who question the establishment are either muzzled or ostracized. We are often given a heartbreaking choice: to live in and develop our true identity or to have acceptance, belonging, and "love" from our family and friends. Many choose to sacrifice the former to receive the later because we are wired for connection. We are wired with a deep need to be accepted into a tribe, and the threat of losing relationships is a loss that many cannot face. What they don't realize is that the very relationships they are sacrificing so much to keep are the very thing that is killing their soul - and their spirit. The longer one stays in a religiously abusive environment, the deeper the lies about who God is and what He is like burrow into your soul, making it harder and harder to break free.

Then there are some who make the sacrifice, who are willing to release anything and everything that is keeping them bound, imprisoned, shackled - including family and friend relationships. It takes an immense amount of courage, and it is incredibly painful, but so worth it. When we release all ties that bind and press into the true, real God, He heals us and restores all that we lost.

The list of lies and distortions of God's character could go on, but the key takeaway here is that the enemy will use whatever he can to distort our view of God so that we cannot understand our true identity as children of God.

Strategy Two: Distort and Twist How We See Ourselves.

When the foundation of who God is is effectively eroded, it makes it much easier for Satan to come in with lies about our personal identity to get us into shame, condemnation, and pride. Many of these lies about our identity are based on lies about God - they are the natural extension of those beliefs. If God is distant, it's because I am a worm, unfit to be noticed by Him. If God's love and acceptance hinges on my behavior, my value is based on what I do but also I cannot be perfect so I will never be good enough which means I will never be fully accepted which either means that I am forever striving or I just give up. Other lies like I am broken, unwanted, unloved, abandoned, and more can all be connected back to an inaccurate belief about God and how He relates to us.

Common Lies We Believe About Our Identity

Following are a few of the most common lies we tend to develop about our identity. It is by no means an exhaustive list - if you want to do a deeper study on the other lies we believe there are plenty of resources out there. For the purposes of this teaching I simply want to touch on the ones I have come across the most.

Lie 1: I am unworthy, broken, abandoned, and/or unwanted

One of the most prevalent lies we can believe about ourselves is that we are broken and unworthy. This one is so pernicious[5] and can be such a hard one to address because on one hand, in our unredeemed state, we are broken and unworthy of God's blessings. It is our very brokenness that Jesus came to heal, and we cannot receive His redemption until we acknowledge our brokenness. BUT once we have received Christ's sacrifice, we are no longer broken. Part of the work of the cross was to make us worthy and to heal us of our brokenness. God is very clear that we are not to call unclean that which He has made clean, and we are not to put in bondage those that He has set free.

Bad theology that has infiltrated the church wants to convince us that even after we have received Christ we are still broken, unworthy sinners. But that couldn't be further from the truth. The Bible is incredibly clear that once we are in Christ we are victorious. That once we have received Christ, we are imbued with ALL the same power and authority and healing as Christ. Jesus came to heal the broken hearted, set the captives free, and declare those who are unloved to be loved. He came so that we might be adopted into the family of God, and we are made co-heirs (read: EQUALS) with Christ in the Kingdom. Through his blood we have access to God, and to all the resources found in Him. But we have to believe and receive in order to experience the fullness of these benefits in Christ.

Lie 2: I am what I do - I have to earn X

Building on the lie of unworthiness, we tend to believe that the way we become worthy is through our works. That we have to earn God's love and acceptance and blessing. But once again this is such a lie. The beauty of the Cross is that it is a FREE gift to all who will accept it. And the victory over sin and death was established once and for all by the Blood of the Lamb. There is literally nothing you can do to earn salvation, and the whole point of salvation is that we are made right with God. We are washed clean so that we can stand worthy in the presence of the Lord.

---

[5] having a harmful effect, especially in a gradual or subtle way

Lie 3: I'm not that bad

Conversely, we also can fall into the self-righteous trap of comparing ourselves to other people, minimizing our own state of sin. We can look at ourselves and then others, focusing on their sin to make us feel better about our own. This is the trap of the Pharisees, the hallmark of the religious spirit. Ironically, it can also hold hands with the previous lie, that we have to earn and prove our worth. Because if we are feeling insecure and like an undeserving worm, what better way to feel better than to find someone who we think is more screwed up and dirtier than us?

Reflection Questions

Do you recognize any of these lies in your own heart and view of yourself? If so, which ones?

Personally, I struggled with all three of these lies at once. The result was that for years, I lived my life in fear and stress. Fear of failing, fear of disappointing Him, fear of accidentally messing up and getting punished. The quiet judgments I held in my heart against those that I would measure myself up against trying to make myself feel better and more worthy contaminated my ability to have close, deep friendships. Fear, isolation, and unprocessed trauma kept me frozen, stuck, and in a constant state of dysregulation that became depression, anxiety, and other mental health struggles. I was constantly overwhelmed, unable to enjoy life fully.

I would pray, but it felt like it was hit and miss if those prayers were heard. I lived in a constant state of striving - I worked SO HARD to be perfect, to be who I THOUGHT a "good

Christian woman/girl" was supposed to look like. I deeply desired to be connected to God, to please Him, to honor Him, but I constantly felt disconnected and like I was failing Him miserably. I spent YEARS crying out to Him, begging Him to fix me and help me be who He wanted me to be.

What I didn't realize in that season is that He didn't design me to fit a mold, He created me to break them. And that by trying to fit the mold, I was suppressing and rejecting the very person He made me to be, thereby rendering my own prayers ineffective by my own choices, born out of my limiting and erroneous[6] beliefs about God's character and heart.

It wasn't until I began to be challenged in my understanding of God's heart and character, as well as given the space and resources to heal the deep wounds I carried, that things shifted. The Lord brought wonderful people into my life to show me who He REALLY is and to shatter the boxes the church and home I grew up in tried to shove Him (and me!) into.

I began to understand and truly KNOW and EXPERIENCE His true character.

I learned, and felt, of His mercy. The balance between justice and grace that is so hard to define in human terms.

I connected with Him. I learned to hear His voice again, and discovered what it looked like to be in tune with Him.

I saw my prayers get answered, and received revelation of the why behind some of those answers.

I started to see healing in my life and the lives of my husband and children.

Depression broke off.

Anxiety broke off.

---

[6] Wrong, incorrect

Shame and fear broke off.

Bitterness and unforgiveness broke off.

Other mental health struggles shifted and eventually healed.

And then.

AND THEN

I started to understand my identity. Not just understand, but embrace and walk in it. I stopped trying to fit into the cage my family of origin and childhood religion had tried to force me into. I developed clarity, confidence, and a strength that I never imagined I could possess. My home became more peaceful as my outer world began to reflect the peace and joy of the Lord that is within me. All because my eyes were opened to where my view of God was inaccurate, and those lies were exchanged for truth. That was the starting point. The place where my life started to change.

It didn't change overnight - it's taken almost a decade to break off the old and step into the new - and I'm by no means perfect or "arrived" yet. But I am healed and on the path of continual growth, not the hamster wheel of perpetual struggles. All because I exchanged the lies that I was believing about God for the Truth.

Part of why this process took so long was because there was an even deeper and more intense attack the enemy had launched against my view of God and myself - and I'm not the only one who has had to face these demons.

Identity Distortion Through Trauma-Induced Soul Fragmentation

One of the enemy's favorite tactics that causes us to question God and undermine our sense of self is trauma and trauma-induced soul fragmentation. Now, I know that "trauma" has become an overused buzz word lately, which has caused many people to dismiss it whenever it is mentioned. However, because trauma is highly subjective, to dismiss all claims of trauma is not a healthy way to correct the issue of overuse. We need to learn what trauma is and engage with those who claim to be traumatized in a compassionate way that leads to healing while also lovingly holding them accountable for their choices. Trauma is a highly subjective thing because it is simply a hard and painful experience that the person does not have the mental or emotional maturity or capacity to process. If a person lacks a healthy support system that can help them process the experience, that trauma will shape the brain and cause it to be stuck in a state of hyper-vigilance, emotional dysregulation, and other unhealthy coping habits.

Some people are so traumatized that they are stuck in their automatic responses but they want to heal and change and are willing to actually do the work required to receive their healing. Those people need us to come alongside them with compassionate, patient, gracious, healthy, trauma-informed, and Biblical support, encouragement, and accountability as they pursue healing. Then there are other people who will use trauma as an excuse to stay in immature and toxic behavior. These people often also have real trauma but are unwilling to do the work that healing requires, instead demanding that people accommodate their toxic behavior because of what was done to them. In those cases it is perfectly acceptable to refuse to get sucked into their victim story but to rather hold them accountable for the choices they are making now, because while one cannot control what happens to them, they are one hundred percent responsible for how they act afterwards.

To discern between the two, we need to rely on the Holy

Spirit for guidance. Due to variables of personality, background, and resources, what is traumatizing for one person isn't always traumatizing for someone else. Everyone has experienced some form of trauma at some point in their life, everyone develops their own protective coping mechanisms to deal with it, and everyone's healing journey, timeline, and process looks different.

Despite the variables of personality, experience, and background, we are all born in the image of God, with an openness to His voice and a strong sense of who we are. It is through our experience of the world that our identity gets tainted. Emotional wounds, traumas, and experiences of this broken world cause us to shrink back, hide, and alter ourselves in order to protect ourselves and feel safe and/or accepted by those around us. Everyone experiences these struggles to some degree throughout their lives, and if left unaddressed, these experiences build and build until a person has lost all sense of their core identity.

In extreme cases, intense and/or ongoing trauma can cause disassociation and soul splits, which is when our soul/personality/mind breaks or fragments into 2 or more pieces, with each broken off piece holding the trauma that created it, along with lies about God or ourselves and parts of our personality. This happens because the brain is unable to process the pain of what the person is experiencing and lacks the support it needs to help it process. God built in this protective mechanism because without it the brain would literally die from overwhelm and pain when faced with extreme trauma. However, He also intended for us to have support and to grow up and develop the ability to process and heal, but so many people are unable to due to lack of understanding, knowledge, and/or healthy support. Unhealed soul fragmentation leads to a host of struggles throughout one's life.

Depending on how soul fragmentation manifests in one's life, the world of psychology has a variety of diagnoses for it. Some of the most common are Schizophrenia, Dissociative Identity Disorder, and Bipolar Disorder, though there are others. While professional psychological support can be beneficial, and even necessary, in many cases, it also has its limits - most notably that psychology says that while one can manage the symptoms of these types of mental health struggles, there is no cure. However our God is the great physician, and He can heal everything, including Schizophrenia, Bipolar, Dissociative Identity Disorder, or any other mental health concerns for that matter. As a matter of fact, the Bible says that Jesus came to heal the broken-hearted (Luke 4:18) - and heart is a word commonly used in Scripture interchangeably for soul. So another way to read that verse is that Jesus came to heal the broken-souled.

Note: Please do NOT read this as an agreement with the extremely damaging teaching from some sects of the church that claim all mental health issues are sin issues and that psychology is not to be trusted and you just need to see a Biblical Counselor. That teaching is wrong, and has caused so much harm. While seeing a Biblical Counselor may be helpful in some situations, unless they also have at least some training in psychology, most are nowhere near adequately equipped to help with serious mental health issues. If you have been diagnosed with ANY mental health concern or suspect you may have a serious mental health concern, you absolutely should be getting professional psychological support.

If you already are, please hear me: I am NOT saying that you should stop seeing your therapist, psychologist, or other licensed mental health professional. You should continue to get that support for as long as you need it. What I ***am*** *saying is that healing is our birthright as followers of Jesus, and that includes mental health. Additionally, most mental health issues do have a spiritual component that needs to be addressed in order to receive your full healing.*

We are three part beings: Body, Soul, and Spirit, and all three of those components need to be addressed, supported, and healed when we are stepping into our identity as healed and whole followers of Christ. So it is a both/and; I highly recommend seeing a mental health professional (ideally Christian) for professional clinical support AND working with a trustworthy Biblically grounded prayer/deliverance/inner healing coach, counselor, or minister AND taking steps to improve/maintain your physical health. All three components need to be in balance in order to be healthy.

I know this on a deeply personal level because I've experienced this type of brokenness in my soul, and I've not only been healed myself but I've had the privilege of being used by God as an instrument in the healing of others. At one point in my life I had well over a dozen soul-fragments that had broken off and held trauma. Just think for a moment about what that does to one's identity - to have 12 or more distinct voices in one's head, each with their own personality and perspective that are often opposite from each other, vying to be the dominant one. That creates such a confusion and crisis of identity. It caused me to get stuck in confusion - who am I? What do I actually want? How am I supposed to engage with the world around me?

It also dulled my ability to hear the Lord's voice because His voice became just another voice in the crowd. I felt so lost, broken, confused, and frustrated because I knew the Lord and I knew that what I was experiencing was not His intention but I couldn't figure out how to get free. These soul fragments caused me to be double minded, lacking any sort of consistency or clear direction because I was quite literally being pulled in every direction. Making a decision felt impossible because I had no idea what my preferences, or even at times convictions, were. Yet no one around me really knew what was going on because I was in an environment that didn't acknowledge mental health struggles as real disorders that need professional support.

In the culture I was raised in, if someone showed symptoms of mental health issues, they were sent to "Biblical Counseling" where they were emotionally beat up with Scriptures taken out of context and shamed into masking their issues. Many ended up leaving the church, or secretly seeing a real mental health professional which only amplified the shame they felt in church. Because of this, I hid and masked my struggles, making it appear like I had it all together. This added a whole new layer of identity crisis, as I felt like a sham, a fake, a pretender - and I was in some ways.

Then the Lord brought me to people who were able to see through the facade and help me bring the trauma, pain, and suppressed memories to the surface so that I could face them, process them, and let the Lord heal them. As I faced the things I had hidden from myself for so long, it broke me in a new way. A good way. It drove me to my knees on a whole new level, causing me to seek the Lord like never before. It forced me to expose and confront things that I had hidden from myself, and that exposure brought full, real healing on that soul level. I experienced every single one of those soul fragments re-integrating into one whole, healed, delivered soul that is fully redeemed, free, and yielded to Christ.

I am so grateful to the Lord for this healing, because being stuck in identity crisis, confusion, and pain renders one totally ineffective for the Kingdom. How can you effectively help someone else heal if you are in the exact same pit? This is why identity work is so important, and why the enemy works so hard to hinder it. But God doesn't play favorites, so what He has done for me, He will do for you if you genuinely ask Him and surrender to the process of healing.

Other Ways Trauma Distorts Our View of God and Self

Even if trauma doesn't cause soul-fragmentation, it often will twist and distort what we believe about who God is, as we discussed in earlier chapters. When you have walked through intense pain, it is natural to question where God was in it. When you are raised in an environment that presents God in a certain light, you're rather prone to believe that's how He is. When the people in authority over you place unreasonable expectations on you, punish you harshly, and devalue you, it's hard to really believe that God is different. In order to heal our identity, we have to walk through a process of questioning and un-learning the beliefs about God and ourselves that are not fully accurate.

So, **how** do we overcome it when it is so deeply ingrained into our mindset and habits?

We start by being open and willing to examine our thoughts and beliefs, and willing to shift whatever is not accurate. Then we acknowledge that there is a disconnect between our beliefs and the Truth. We discover where that disconnect is, how it occurred, address any traumas, and then realign our beliefs with the Truth (which usually requires inner healing, forgiveness, and deliverance). Then, we start walking in the Truth, building ourselves up in our most holy faith by renewing our minds consistently with God's word and spending time in His presence.

But sometimes this is easier said than done because the wounds which created the disconnect run so deep and are so painful. It feels hard and scary to even admit they exist. That's where a Holy-Spirit led Coach/Mentor like myself and others listed in the resource section can come in. We walk with you (and guide you as needed) through the process of discovering, processing, and releasing the things that are keeping you stuck, feeling disconnected from God, confused, and hurting.

Reflection Questions

Do you recognize some of the symptoms of soul splits in yourself? (On top of what was listed above, symptoms can include mood swings, large blackouts in your childhood memories - not having clear or distinct memories after age 3, memories that you have the start of but suddenly go black and you can't remember how it ends, walking into a room and forgetting why you are there, losing a thought mid sentence, intense internal conflict, automatic responses that feel so out of character for who you really are/want to be, and more)

If so, or if you suspect or know that you may have trauma in your past or present, I strongly encourage you to reach out to one of the coaches listed in the resource section at the end of the book.

PART THREE

WHAT DOES GOD AND HIS WORD SAY ABOUT WHO HE IS AND WHO WE ARE

Every single one of the wrong beliefs and lies we've explored (as well as countless more) opens the door for the enemy to mess with us. Coming into agreement with these lies is coming into agreement with the enemy and gives him an open door to oppress and sometimes even possess space within our soul. (Yes, even Christians can be possessed. I've personally witnessed it, been delivered, and delivered others in the name of Jesus). So as we are in the process of learning the Truth about God's character and identity, we will often need deliverance and inner healing to help align our actions with our new beliefs. The best place to start is to clarify what God's Word says about who He is and who we are.

Who is God

Scripture is full of God describing Himself to us, as well as people ascribing names to Him based on their experience of Him. There are at least 100 of these names, and every single one of them is well worth studying. However, since there are several books out there devoted just to studying the names of God, for what we are discussing here we are just going to look at just a few of the names and characteristics of God most relevant to the topic at hand.

For those who have lots of experience in the religious world, you may read the following names and characteristics of God with a sense of apathy. You may feel like you already know this, you've heard it in church and at conferences and online and all the things for most of your life. But if you're still reading this book, odds are you have experienced and/or believed some of the painful things I've exposed in the previous sections, and therefore there is a disconnect between you and God. May I suggest that this disconnect may partly be because your head knowledge has not become heart knowledge? If you find yourself wanting to skim, shut down, or even skip this section, don't. Really sit with these names and characteristics of God. Read the scripture references. Then dig in and find out more about what the Word says about God. Let Him reveal Himself to you on a heart level.

Almighty, Powerful, and Lord Over All

The very first name for God found in the Bible is Elohim "The Strong Creator God" (Genesis 1:1-2). From the very first verse of the very first book in Scripture, God clearly reveals Himself as the most high God above all others, creator of all that was, is, and is to come. Later, God also reveals that His name is YHWH - "I am" - the self existent one. Most famously found in Exodus when giving Moses his commission from the burning bush (Exodus 3:14), this name for God is used throughout Scripture over 6,000 times. Building on this, He is also called Adonai, which means "Lord or Master over All" (Genesis 15:2) and El Elyon which means "The Most High God" (Deuteronomy 26:19). He is acknowledged as the judge over all the earth (Psalm 58:11), and frequently referred to as El Shaddai "Almighty God" (Genesis 17:1).

God is the ultimate authority in the universe. He is all powerful, mighty, and sovereign over all. That much is certain, it is clearly established throughout Scripture. However, as we discussed in earlier chapters, He is not like the flawed authority figures we experience here on earth. He is perfect, holy, and good. He is also deeply relational.

Relational, Intimate, and Connected Father who is our Refuge, Redeemer, and Protector

In the New Testament we see God referred to as Abba "Father" frequently (see Mark 14:36, Romans 8:15, and Galatians 4:6 for example). However, He reveals Himself as a loving Father all through the Old Testament as well. In Genesis, He reveals Himself to Hagar (Sarah's Egyptian slave, concubine of Abraham, and mother of Ishmael) in a deeply personal, caring, and loving way, and she calls Him El-Roi "The God who Sees Me" (Genesis 16:13). Another name for God found over 7,000 times in the Scriptures is Jehovah "Lord, Master, and Relational God". God's very name indicates His desire for relationship with us. God also refers to Himself as Jehovah Kanna Shemo "The Lord Whose Name is Jealous" (Exodus 34:14). He loves and desires us so much that He gets jealous when we choose other things over Him, and ultimately He will not tolerate competition. We have the freedom to choose Him, but if we do, we must choose Him and Him alone. He will not compete for our affections. This principle is illustrated many times in Scripture through the metaphor of marriage with God being a husband and His people (Israel and the Church) being the Bride. Just as a man does not want a wife who flirts and sleeps around with other men, so too does God not want people who entertain and engage with other gods (idols).

Of course one of His most famous relational names is Immanuel which literally means "God with Us" and is most commonly used in reference to Jesus. However, there are many more descriptions of God as a relational God, especially in the Old Testament. Jeremiah 23:23 calls Him "The God who is Near". Ezekiel calls Him Jehovah Shammah "The Lord was There" (Ezekiel 48:35). Joshua refers to Him as the Living God, and in Judges Gideon is told "The Lord is With You" (Judges 6:12), an encouragement that is commonly given to those who follow the Lord throughout Scripture. All these names and references to God describe a being who is present, connected, and deeply personal.

Additionally, the Psalms (and other books in the Old Testament) are filled with descriptions of God as personal and connected to our individual lives, detailing His love, goodness, and faithfulness. He is described as our defense (Psalm 89:19), our shield (Deuteronomy 33:29), our refuge (Psalm 62:8; 91:1), our fortress (Jeremiah 16:19), our high tower (Psalm 18:2), and our rock (2 Samuel 22:47), just to name a few. He is also described as a shepherd, a helper, and a kinsman-redeemer.

All of these names work together to paint a picture of His desire for an intimate, connected relationship with His people. He loves us, and desires real relationships, not mindless slaves.

Our Vindicator, Victory, and Provider

One of the most comforting characteristics of God for those of us who have experienced abuse or injustice of any kind is that He is our vindicator. In Psalm 18:47 He is called El Nekamoth the "God that Avenges" and this picture of God as the avenger, defender, and provider of His people is one of the most frequently presented in Scripture. He is also described as the God of Recompense (Jeremiah 51:56), as He not only avenges us but He provides compensation to us for the loss and pain we have endured.

Not only does He avenge, vindicate, and provide recompense, God is also Jehovah Nissi "The Lord my Banner" as in the banner of victory that is raised after winning a battle. He is the God of hosts (Psalm 59:5), mighty in battle (Psalm 24:8). He is a consuming fire (Deuteronomy 4:24), ready to consume those who oppose Him and come against His beloved people. He fights for and alongside us, guaranteeing victory to those who are in alignment with Him. He is Jehovah Jireh, the "God who Provides" (Genesis 22:14). This provision encompasses all areas - physical, emotional, spiritual - the Lord God owns the earth and the fullness thereof, and He provides all the resources we need to execute our assignments when we are walking in alignment with Him. That last phrase is key to understand: God's promises of protection, provision, and blessing only apply to when we are walking in obedience, as He cannot bless disobedience.

Our Healer, Peace, Righteousness, and Sanctification

Some of my personal favorite names of God are Jehovah Rapha "The Lord Our Healer", Jehovah Shalom "The Lord our Peace", and Jehovah Tsidkenu "The Lord our Righteousness". Just think about these names for a minute. GOD is the source of our healing, peace, and righteousness. Not only that, but GOD is the one who sanctifies us as well (Exodus 31:13). Emphasis on GOD - HE is the one who does the work, the heavy lifting in these scenarios. He is our Savior through His son Jesus, our source of strength, and our light guiding the way to life. All we have to do is go to Him through the Blood of the Lamb, believe, and receive His love and work in us with praise and thanksgiving.

For Further Study: Other Names and Characteristics

Here are just a few more names and characteristics of God. I encourage you to meditate on them, find them in the Scriptures for yourself, and let yourself really soak in WHO God is.

He is:

- Holy (Joshua 24:19)
- Faithful (Deuteronomy 7:9)
- Kind - it is His kindness that leads us to repentance (Romans 2:4)!
- Glorious (Psalm 29:3)
- God of our Life (Psalm 42:8)
- King (Psalm 68:24)
- Source of Joy (Psalm 43:4)
- Our Salvation (Psalm 51:14)
- Our Strength (2 Samuel 22:33)
- Our Praise (Psalm 109:1)
- Merciful (Psalm 59:10)
- Everlasting (Psalm 48:14)

These are just a few. The Scripture is FULL of descriptions of who God is, both that He provides Himself, and from people who had real encounters with Him. While of course the New Testament has amazing information about Jesus and revelations about the Father through Him, the Old Testament, especially the prophets, are rich resources for gaining a better understanding of God's heart and character.

Application/Reflection

Which of the names/characteristics of God resonate with you the most?

Why?

Which of the names/characteristics of God do you struggle with the most?

Why?

I strongly encourage you to do a deep study of the names of God in the Bible, making sure to invite the Holy Spirit in to teach and heal you with His word.

The Triune Nature of God

One other thing about God that must be addressed is what theology calls His "Triune Nature". Tons of theology books have been written on this subject, and the details of the meaning of "Triune" and all that are the topics of heavy debate and can get really complicated really fast - if that's something you want to study deeper, please do so. As I have mentioned several times, this is not meant to be a big scholarly treatise, it is simply me acting in obedience to the Lord's call to share what He has taught me on this concept of identity through my personal experience and study. That being said, let me share as simple of an explanation of the Trinity as I can, as I have come to understand it.

God is a three-part being (so are we for that matter, that's part of being made in the image of God - but I'll get to that later on when we talk about the Truth of our identity). He exists as a three-part being with each part being a distinct person with His own mind, will, emotions, and role that they play in the Godhead and in the universe overall. These persons are God the Father, God the Son, and God the Holy Spirit. One Being, three parts or persons. As I mentioned, each person has a distinct role within the One True God and how He engages with His creation:

God the Father

God the Father operates as the Head, the Supreme Authority, the Judge, the Commander, the King, the Creator. It is God the Father who is seated on the throne of ruling and judgement rendering verdicts and edicts in the Throne Room. God the Father is the part of God who holds time in His hands, and decides the days, times, and hours of all creation. It is God the Father that most people think of when they think of God, and God the Father operates in most of the attributes we have already discussed - provider, vindicator, shepherd, healer, refuge, etc. although those attributes apply to the whole Trinity as well.

It is God the Father who often gets a bad rap for being harsh, controlling, and more. Often, when people believe lies about God, those lies are primarily about the part of God that is identified in the Bible as God the Father. This issue has been around for centuries, as 20th century preacher Samuel Chadwick observes in his compilation of sermons entitled "Humanity and God":

> A false theology has slandered and caricatured God by representing Him as a relentless Shylock[7] grimly exacting extreme penalty from an innocent Son. The result is that the Son is loved and the Father feared. The unspoken creed of many is summed up in the words: "I love Jesus, but I fear God." The story is told of a Christian worker who was shocked at the answer received from a dying widow to the assurance of God's fatherly care for the widow and the fatherless. The dying woman raised herself upon her bed and entreated: "Do not talk about God. I am afraid of God. I hate God. Every hard and bitter thing in my life has come from God." Quietly the exhausted woman was allowed to recover strength. Then the Christian began to speak of Jesus. "Ah! yes," said the dying woman, "He's different, isn't He? He was so good and kind. I like to hear about Him. I could trust Him."

This "false theology" unfortunately is still going strong today, which robs so many believers of the power, strength, authority, joy, peace, and beauty that comes from truly knowing who God is and living in intimate communion with Him - ALL of Him - the

---

[7] Shylock is the antagonist of Shakespeare's play The Merchant of Venice. He is a Jewish moneylender, shown as a complex character who has become bitter due to suffering from prejudice and racism at the hands of Christians. He requests a "pound of flesh" as collateral for a loan from a Christian merchant in the play, which leads to his downfall and forced conversion to Christianity. Now this term is used as a racial anti-semitic slur or as a derogatory term for someone who lends money at an excessive rate of interest.

whole Trinity. Because God the Father and Jesus are one. God the Father, Jesus, and Holy Spirit are one, and because they are one, you cannot truly love, know, and have a relationship with Him if you only engage with and focus on one part or aspect of Him.

<u>Reflection Questions</u>

Do you resonate with the dying woman in the story?

Do you find yourself afraid of God, thinking of Him as harsh and controlling, therefore choosing to avoid Him, and focusing on other things that feel safer?

Do you find yourself interacting with the three persons of God as if they were three different beings rather than distinct parts of one whole?

Are you willing to open yourself to the possibility that your perspective on Him is incorrect and open to opportunities to develop evidence for God's true character?

God the Son

God the Son operates as the physical manifestation of God on earth to humans, as well as the part by which God the Father created all things and through whom He brings salvation to the world. In the Old Testament, we see God the Son show up as The Angel of the Lord who appears to several people, including Abraham, Joshua, and Zechariah. We know this entity to be God the Son because He is the only "angel" who accepts the worship of those who see Him. All other "angels" in the Bible correct the humans if they bow in worship and clearly communicate that they are not God. God the Son is most recognizable from the New Testament when He enters the world as Jesus Christ, Yeshua Ha Mashiach, the Word made flesh,

Immanuel - God with us.

The perfect Son of God chose to also become a son of man, wholly human and wholly divine. He entered the world to experience all that it means to be human, navigate it sinlessly, and then give His life freely in exchange for ours that we may be redeemed and freed from our brokenness and sin. It is through God the Son that salvation is available to us, so He operates as our Savior, our Sustainer, our Prince of Peace, Wonderful Counselor, Firstborn among many brethren (i.e. US - Romans 8:29), and our Friend (John 15:15). He also operates as our advocate and mediator before the Father, our high priest who understands us because He became one of us.

It is crucial to understand the identity of Jesus because the Bible clearly tells us that once we have received salvation, our old identity is removed and we are given a new identity in Christ. Part of that new identity is that we become like Christ, and that all the attributes of His character, power, and authority are placed on us. Christ Himself promises that *". . . the one who believes in me will also do the works that I do.* ***And he will do even greater works than these****, because I am going to the Father*" (John 14:12, CSB, emphasis mine). Later on in 1 John 4:17 we are told that ". . . as he [Christ] is, so also are we in this world" (CSB) - and this literally means that all the power, authority, wisdom, access to resources, EVERYTHING that Christ is, we also are and have access to RIGHT NOW. (If you're struggling with that one, don't worry, I did too - that story and a deeper explanation is coming up shortly).

<u>Reflection Questions</u>
Do you have a personal relationship with Jesus?

Do you intimately know and understand who He is, and who He is to you?

God the Holy Spirit

God the Holy Spirit operates as the seal of our salvation, the literal indwelling of God in us, our direct communication line from earth to heaven. The Holy Spirit enters into us when we accept Christ, and it is through the Holy Spirit that we are empowered to align our lives with Christ. The Holy Spirit comforts, teaches, guides, reveals, convicts, and interacts with us. He is the helper promised by Christ before His resurrection and ascension:

> *And I will ask the Father, and he will give you another Counselor, to be with you forever. He is the Spirit of truth. The world is unable to receive him because it doesn't see him or know him. But you do know him, because he remains with you and will be in you. . . "I have spoken these things to you while I remain with you. But the Counselor, the Holy Spirit, whom the Father will send in my name, will teach you all things and remind you of everything I have told you.*
> - John 14:16–7; 25-26, CSB

It is through the Holy Spirit that we receive the gifts of the Spirit to be used to further the Kingdom of God. These gifts include words of wisdom, words of knowledge, supernatural healing, faith, prophecy, the discerning of spirits, speaking in tongues (not to be confused with a private prayer language), and the interpretation of those tongues (1Corinthians 12:7-11). They also include generosity, acts of service, teaching, exhorting, leading, and mercy, to name a few.

It seems appropriate here to address one of the most pernicious lies that has permeated a large percentage of the Church - the Western Church especially - the lie of the doctrine of Cessationism. Cessationism is the belief that all the "charismatic" or "supernatural" gifts of the Holy Spirit (such as speaking in tongues, prophecy, healing, and words of knowledge) ceased - stopped, ended - with the closing of the cannon of the Bible at the Council of Trent in 1546 A.D.

This doctrine uses 1 Corinthians 13:8-10 to support this idea. *". . . But as for prophecies, they will come to an end; as for tongues, they will cease; as for knowledge, it will come to an end. For we know in part, and we prophesy in part, but when the perfect comes, the partial will come to an end."* Those who teach the doctrine of cessationism claim that the "perfect" referred to in this passage is the Bible. They say that because the Bible is the infallible (incapable of making mistakes) and inerrant (incapable of being wrong) Word of God, once the cannon of the Bible was closed, all need for direct or additional revelation from the Lord was ended. Cessationists also use Revelation 22:18 to support their stance. According to this passage *"I [the Apostle John] testify to everyone who hears the words of the prophecy of this book: If anyone adds to them, God will add to him the plagues that are written in this book."* They say that this verse applies to the whole cannon of Scripture, and that anyone claiming to have a fresh revelation or word of prophecy from the Lord after the closing of the cannon is a false prophet and a heretic.

I am deeply familiar with this doctrine because the "Christian" culture I was raised in was militantly devoted to it. We had books on books and classes on classes focused on promoting this teaching. The president of the "Christian" college I attended was one of the foremost teachers and promoters of this ideology. As a matter of fact, while I was a student, he released a book (one of multiple of his career) focused on not just promoting Cessationism, but also attacking those who disagree. I personally was required to take a Bible class where a large chunk of our time was spent by the teacher drilling into us the evils of the Charismatics who believe that all the gifts of the Spirit still exist. However, there was very little actual Scripture used to support that point (because there isn't any that can stand up to critical thinking and being read in the full context of Scripture) so at one point in that class I made an appointment with my teacher to ask him about it, because when I read the passages that talk about the gifts of the Spirit, they seemed to point to the conclusion that all the gifts are available and active to this day. His response was the argument I have previously shared - that the Bible is the "perfect" referred to in 1 Corinthians 13:10, and since we have perfect revelation in the

Bible, there is no need for prophecy or tongues or miracles.

This is just plain wrong. Firstly, if you read the full context of the passage (especially verse 12), the "perfect" mentioned in 1 Corinthians 13:10 is obviously referring to our glorified life with Christ. Secondly, there are many passages throughout the New Testament that talk about how to use the gifts of the Spirit properly, which implies they must exist and be in use if such instructions are necessary. Additionally, Jesus Himself affirms that His followers will have access to the same supernatural and miraculous power as He did, and that we will do greater works than Him here on earth because of the authority He has given us (John 14:12). Finally, Cessationism contradicts a clear Biblical principle found in both the Old and New Testaments that God does not change. He is the same yesterday, today, and forever. This means that if He worked through miracles and supernatural signs a thousand years ago, He does the same today. To claim that the supernatural gifts no longer exist is to say that God has changed.

Ultimately, the only way to support the Cessationist belief is to cherry pick specific Scriptures and interpret them out of context (which violates key Hermeneutic[8] principles for Scripture interpretation). We've already seen this in the analysis of the 1 Corinthians passage, but let's also address the passage in Revelation. Cessationists claim that Revelation 22:18 applies to the whole canon of Scripture. They point to the fact that Revelation is the final book of the canon and Revelation 22:18 is part of the final extortion of that final book. Therefore, they say, it should apply to all that came before in the entire canon, and is evidence that there is no need for modern day prophets. However, this is once again incorrect. When John wrote Revelation, there was no official canon for the Christian Bible, and the message He was delivering was a very specific one received directly from the resurrected and ascended Christ from Heaven regarding the Church age and the end of days.

---

[8] Hermeneutics is the method or theory of interpretation. Biblical Hermeneutics follow four key principles: context (historical, cultural, etc.), authorial intent, genre, and using Scripture to interpret Scripture.

Therefore, the warning against adding anything to “the words of the prophecy of this book” is specifically referring to the prophetic words contained in the book of Revelations. It is not saying that God is done speaking to His people!

Ultimately, Cessationism is a demonic, blasphemous doctrine that strips the Church of access to her source of power and authority. You can tell by the fruit - there is a lack of Spiritual fruit in the lives and churches of those who believe this doctrine. There is little to none of the true joy, freedom, or peace we are promised as believers! This doctrine feeds the Spirit of Religion which burdens people with rules and regulations without relationship, law without true love. Even now as I am writing I can feel the Father’s frustration and indignation at how these people twist His word and lead His people astray! Those who partner with Religion are harsh, critical, unloving, and judgmental. Those who are under it are filled with shame, fear, and even despair. Christ came to free us from all that, so why do we tolerate teachers who put us back under a burden?

Reflection Questions
Have you been taught, or do you hold to the Cessationist view of the Gifts of the Spirit?

If so, are you willing to genuinely explore the possibility of that view being incorrect and be open to looking at other perspectives and experiences?

The Seven Spirits/Attributes of God

The Holy Spirit is not only the conduit through whom we as believers receive our power, authority, and understanding, He was also the source of Jesus’ power when He was on earth. Throughout the Scriptures He is described with seven key attributes. These attributes are also sometimes called the Seven Spirits of God. Some people say these Seven Spirits are simply attributes of the Holy Spirit, others believe that these Seven Spirits are their own distinct entities that come forth from God. Personally, I am not sure which one is accurate, and I'm not entirely sure how much it matters in the big picture. The main thing is that these Spirits/Attributes are clearly presented in Scripture as Spirits belonging to God. Since this book is not really meant to be a theological deep dive, we are just going to focus on the core point of what the goal and purpose of these Spirits/Attributes are and how they impact us.

The seven spirits/attributes are most clearly summarized in Isaiah: "Then a shoot will grow from the stump of Jesse, and a branch from his roots will bear fruit. The Spirit of the Lord will rest on him— a Spirit of wisdom and understanding, a Spirit of counsel and strength, a Spirit of knowledge and of the fear of the Lord" (Isaiah 11:2), however these seven spirits are referenced in other passages such as Revelation 1:4, 4:5, and 5:6, and Zechariah 3:9. The shoot Isaiah 11:2 references is Jesus (and we as believers are the branches), and the rest of the verse clearly lists seven spirits/attributes:

The Spirit of the Lord

It is through the Spirit of the Lord that Jesus operated in the power of God, and how we receive the power of God. It is through this Spirit that God's people are empowered to perform miracles, prophesy, and walk in the authority He has given them. It is through the Spirit of the Lord that we learn about and experience the reality of the Kingdom of Heaven[9].

The Spirit of Wisdom

It is through the Spirit of Wisdom that we are able to gain insight, interpret it correctly, and then apply it wisely, in alignment with God's purposes rather than worldly ones[10]. It is by this spirit that Jesus "grew in wisdom and stature, in favor with both God and Man" (Luke 2:52). This spirit is referred to

---

[9] Umphress, The Seven Spirits of God

[10] Gheorghica, What are the Seven Spirits of God?

consistently throughout the book of Proverbs, and is typically personified as female. We also find a description of the Spirit of Wisdom in James 3:15-17. Wisdom equips us to walk rightly with God.

The Spirit of Understanding

The Spirit of Understanding works with the Spirit of Wisdom to deepen our revelation and knowledge of how the Kingdom works, and how to operate in alignment with it. It is the practical application of the insight Wisdom gives. Discernment is a crucial aspect of this attribute as well, as it allows us to rightly divide what is right and true from what seems so but isn't.

The Spirit of Counsel

This is the attribute of the Spirit that acts as our helper, our counselor, and our personal adviser. It is through this Spirit that we receive direct, specific instruction and direction from God.

The Spirit of Strength

The Spirit of Strength is where we get the supernatural strength to persevere through all things. This is the strength and might of God that empowers us to walk in His way, to stand strong in the face of adversity and opposition, and to walk worthy of the calling He has placed on our lives.

The Spirit of Knowledge

The Spirit of Knowledge is the deep revelation and intimate knowledge of the Lord that equips and empowers us to navigate life on this earth from a place grounded in God. It helps us to operate from a Kingdom, Supernatural, Spiritual perspective rather than a worldly, natural, carnal one.

The Spirit of the Fear of the Lord

The Spirit of the Fear of the Lord is what instills in us a holy reverence and respect for the Lord. It brings the awareness of the holiness of God and gives us a healthy sense of awe at His glory, righteousness, and majesty. Unlike unholy fear, this type of fear draws us closer to God rather than making us run from Him[11]. This holy sense of awe and reverence deepens our desire for relationship with Him, while helping to ensure we approach Him in the appropriate posture.

These Seven Spirits/Attributes along with the Holy Spirit were upon Jesus and the source of His power on earth, which means that we who are in Christ have access to all these attributes as well.

<u>*Reflection Questions*</u>

After reading about all the characteristics of the Holy Spirit, take a moment to really reflect. Are you walking in the fullness of the Holy Spirit power that is available to you?

If so, how? If not, why?

As we have seen, God has three distinct persons or parts with distinct roles they play among themselves and the universe. Despite being three distinct persons, they are one being or entity, meaning that they all are of one accord, one purpose, and are deeply inter-connected, thereby always operating in complete unity. The names and characteristics of God that we have already discussed apply to all three persons, however as we have discussed these characteristics manifest uniquely in each person of the Trinity.

I share all of this because it is crucial to understand the character and identity of God - all three persons that make Him up - because we are made in His image, and when we accept Christ, we become His sons and daughters. As anyone who has studied biology can tell you, sons and daughters inherit traits from their parents. Just so do we inherit characteristics of our father in heaven. When we are born into the family of God we

[11] Gheorghica, What are the Seven Spirits of God?

are given new gifts, identity, purpose, and characteristics. Not only that, but Scripture clearly teaches that when we accept Christ, we receive His identity. So, in order to understand our identity, we must understand His.

Reflection Questions

Are you engaging with God in His entirety, or are you focusing on just one aspect/part/person of Him?

Who We Are

Biblically, our identity is defined in two key phases: before Christ and after Christ. The enemy loves to get in our heads and convince us that we are our old identity, or that we have somehow lost our new identity, or that we have to work to earn the new identity, or even that what the Bible says about our new identity cannot be taken at face value. All of these are lies, used to keep us stuck, in bondage, and less effective in our calling. It is crucial that we understand the difference between our old identity and our new identity so we can walk in the right one, and stand strong when the enemy tries to get us back into our old identity.

Before (Outside of) Christ - Our Old Identity

The Bible is really clear about who we were before Christ. It is crucial to understand that regardless of whether we have accepted Christ or not, ALL humans are made in the image of God. But what does that mean? It means that we are a reflection of Him here on earth in a few ways. One of those ways is that we are three-part beings just as He is a three part being. We have body, soul, and spirit, and all three of these parts have their own mind, will, and emotions, yet work together to form one person. This is a key concept to understand and work with when working through any sort of healing, because all three parts must be addressed and ministered to in the healing process. Another way we are made in His image is that we are creative and have imagination. No other created being in the heavens or on earth has these characteristics. Additionally we each have unique personalities, consciousness, and intellect on a level that is different from every other living being on earth. All of this works together to make humankind the only type of created being that is made in the image of God.

However, while being made in the image of God automatically imbues every human with value and worth, as well as the potential of greatness, before Christ we had no hope of ever reaching our full potential because we were broken, slaves to sin, incapable of being righteous. We were ruled by our passions and lusts, selfish, prideful, and imagining all kinds of evil. We were idolaters, exchanging the truth about God for a lie (Romans 1:25). According to Romans 1:29-31 we were "filled with all unrighteousness, evil, greed, and wickedness. . . . full of envy, murder, quarrels, deceit, and malice . . . gossips, slanderers, God-haters, arrogant, proud, boastful, inventors of evil, disobedient to parents, senseless, untrustworthy, unloving, and unmerciful" (CSB). According to Ephesians 2:1-3 we were dead in our sin, following the "ruler of the power of the air" (Satan), disobedient, ruled by and "carrying out the inclinations of our flesh and thoughts . . . we were by nature children under wrath" (CSB). As such we deserved the punishment for sin, which is death. This death is not just physical death, it is eternal death in the form of separation from God for eternity.

For those of us who are active in the church, and maybe were raised in the church and/or Christian and/or highly moral homes, it is important to note here, that even if you personally did not physically commit these specifically listed sins, you still have sinned and all of the above paragraph still applies to you. Jesus makes it very clear several times, most famously in the Sermon on the Mount recorded in Matthew, that to even entertain thoughts about committing a sin is to sin. To lust after someone is no different spiritually than actually having illicit sex with them. To hate someone is no different spiritually than actually murdering them. This principle applies to all sin. To judge someone and consider yourself better than them is just as bad as enslaving them and subjecting them. Sin is a heart issue, not an action issue. It is the intention, desire, and thoughts of your heart that determine your righteousness, not your actions. This is made abundantly clear every time Jesus interacted with the Pharisees. They were the religious leaders of the time, and from the outside they appeared clean and righteous. They were fastidious about following the letter of the Law (and even heaped additional rules on top of it), but they missed the heart behind it, and inside were full of pride, self-righteousness, and judgement.

Oh, how sad this is such a perfect description of many churches and Christians today! We boil the Scriptures down to a list of do's and don'ts, and then add more rules on top of it; instead of setting people free from bondage, we simply change the clothes of their bondage from worldly rags to pretty religious chains. This Spirit of the Pharisees, most accurately named the Spirit of Religion, Legalism, and Law, has so pervasively infiltrated the church that it has rendered her ineffective in her mission much of the time. We burden people with rules and judgement, and then we wonder why people are leaving the churches they grew up in, and why outreach and evangelism initiatives fall flat. Jesus came to demolish religion, not establish a new one. He came to restore our relationship with the Father, not to burden us with more rules.

Not only that, but religion cheapens Jesus' sacrifice by causing people to think they are better than they are. They think that if they check all the boxes, they are righteous, worthy, and better than the person who didn't. Checking the boxes feeds pride, blinding the religious to their need for Jesus. Oh, I can feel heartbreak of the Father, and how my heart breaks with His, when I think of how many people religiously attend church, serve, and check all the boxes in the name of Jesus, but when they reach Heaven, will be shocked when they hear the words "I never knew you". I can see so many beautiful souls, standing there, weeping because they thought they were in Christ but they were only in religion. Please do not be one of them. If you are reading this book, I implore you, put down your pride. Invite the Lord to search your heart and remove any unclean thing from within you (Psalm 139:23-24), and truly, deeply, on that deep heart and soul level, surrender to Him! Do not be one who thinks they are written in the Book of Life but are not! Please understand, that just like the Pharisees, if you do not understand the depth of the depravity of who you are before Christ, you may never actually know Him and receive the identity of one who is In Christ.

Application/Reflection Questions

Do you have an accurate view of who you were before/without Christ? (It's important to note that an accurate view inspires emotions of gratitude and worship, not shame or embarrassment)

Have you entertained and operated from a place of self righteousness?

If so, I implore you, repent of it and ask the Lord to cleanse your heart. Ask Him to give you His eyes, that you may see yourself and others the way He does. One of my personal favorite ways to walk through this process is through praying worship songs and scripture that speak to this desire for a clean heart and heavenly perspective.

The bridge of the song "Hosanna" by Hillsong United is one of my favorites to sing as a prayer:

Heal my heart and make it clean
Open up my eyes to the things unseen
Show me how to love like You have loved me
Break my heart for what breaks Yours
Everything I am for Your Kingdom's cause
As I walk from earth into eternity

"Give me Your Eyes" by Brandon Heath, "Be Thou My Vision", and "Turn Your Eyes Upon Jesus" are just a few more of the many wonderful songs out there that speak to transforming our vision from our fleshly perspective to God's Kingdom perspective. If these specific suggestions do not resonate with you, a simple Google search of "Christian songs about Godly vision/seeing through God's eyes" will yield a bounty of options for you. Worship is a key weapon of our warfare, and a very effective tool in shifting our mindset.

After (Or In) Christ - Our New Identity

While Scripture is very clear about our pre-Christ identity, it spends much more time teaching, describing, and empowering us in our in-Christ identity. Right off the bat, there is a clear implication here that once we have accepted Christ our focus should be on looking forward, not looking back. Which makes sense, because where our attention goes, our energy flows. In other words, we go where we are looking. So if we are constantly looking back at who we were before Christ, is it any wonder that we are stuck in the same behaviors and cycles? But when we look forward - at who Christ is and who He is calling us to be - something amazing happens. We begin to transform more and more into His image - we begin to think, act, and speak like Him. So what is our identity in Christ?

When we choose to accept Christ, we choose to become His bondservants. This specific term is used frequently by the Apostles in the New Testament when they are describing their relationship to Christ, and is a perfect description of an aspect of relationship that all believers should have with Him. While some Bible translations use the word "slave", that is not an accurate depiction because it implies force or lack of choice. In the Bible (and throughout history for that matter), there is a difference between slaves and bondservants. Slaves were typically prisoners of war (or their descendants) or people and their families who could not pay their debts who were taken captive and forced to work. However, a bondservant is not just a slave. It is a person who was a slave and was given the opportunity to be free but who chose to remain in the service of that master permanently because he was such a good master. (The guidelines for how this worked are found in Exodus 21:5-6 and Deuteronomy 15:12-18.)

Really think about that. There were actually people who CHOSE a life of servitude because living their lives in service to a good master was better than being free and eking out a living for themselves. These bondservants were life-long servants who CHOSE to serve their master because they loved them. This is the imagery that Paul uses to describe his (and our) relationship with Christ. We have free will. We don't have to serve the Lord. But because of his goodness and kindness and mercy and love, we chose to dedicate our lives to his service. And when we do, he reconciles us with God (Colossians 1:22), and then He changes our status from servant to friend and brother (or sister).

When we choose to become a bondservant, God receives us and then does one better and adopts us, making us His children. In Christ, we are saved, redeemed from the punishment for sin, and made righteous and at peace with God (Romans 5:1). We are made citizens of the Kingdom of Heaven (Ephesians 2:19, Philippians 1:27), set free from bondage to sin (1 Corinthians 3:17, Galatians 5:1), and empowered to live a life of righteousness. More than that, we are children of God (Galatians 3:26) and the recipients of all the benefits thereof. No longer are we just working for the Master, we become His heirs (Galatians 4:7, Ephesians 2:6-7, 19)! We are granted all the same access, authority, privilege, power, and provision as Jesus Christ Himself (John 14:12-13).

As Christ-followers we are a new creation (2 Corinthians 5:17). Stop and think about that for a minute. When you accepted Christ, your old identity died and God gave you a brand new one with all the same characteristics as Jesus! Then, He gave you a mission and a purpose: you are to be salt and light (just like Jesus!) and an ambassador for Christ in this world (Matthew 6:13-16; 2 Corinthians 5:20). To ensure that we are able to carry out our mission, we are empowered with supernatural weapons for spiritual warfare (2 Corinthians 10:3-5, Ephesians 6:10-17), appointed as God's Temple here on earth (1 Corinthians 3:16, Ephesians 2:22), and connected to the Body of Christ for fellowship and mutual support (1 Corinthians 12).

Other descriptions of our new identity in Scripture declare that we are holy, faultless, and blameless before God (Colossians 1:22), alive in Christ where we were previously dead to sin (Ephesians 2:5, Colossians 2:13-14), and brought into the household of God (Hebrews 3:6). 1 Peter 2:9 declares us a chosen race, a royal priesthood, a holy nation, and a peculiar people for Christ's possession. The word peculiar does not mean weird in this context (although when we live fully sold out, surrendered, and obedient to Christ the world tends to think that we are weird). In this context it means that we are unique, special, or set apart.

Scripture is also clear that we have authority (Luke 10:19). But we don't have just any authority, no! We have the same level of power and authority as Jesus Himself. First John 4:17 tells us that "as Christ is, so are we in this world", and Jesus himself says in the Gospel of John 14:12 that "the one who believes in me will also do the works that I do. *And he will do even greater works than these*" (emphasis mine). (Other passages that support this idea are: Matthew 17:20, 21:21-22, Mark 16:15-18, Luke 10:19-20). As believers, we have been imbued (filled, permeated with) with the same power, authority, and access to God through the Holy Spirit as Jesus! This is so crucial to understand, because it is the key to actually experiencing the victory that is already there. You just have to walk in it!

But here's the deal: we only have access to these things when we are truly in Christ. Truly in Christ. To be truly in Christ means that we are actively walking with Him, surrendering our will to His, and obeying His instructions (1 John 1:3-6). Many of the promises and opportunities of God (outside of salvation) are conditional - IF we obey, THEN we will experience God's power and glory. Jesus clearly says, "If you love me you will obey my commands" (John 14:15). We are not in Christ if we are not obeying Him. We are not saved by our actions, but our actions prove that we are in Christ. Scripture is clear that the evidence of our salvation is a changed life - not due to checking religious boxes but because our very hearts and desires have changed because of our intimacy with Christ.

Clarifying and really understanding who we are in Christ is crucial to breaking free from religion and legalism because we don't do things in order TO BE right with God, we do things because we ALREADY ARE right with God. It's all about the heart. The motivation comes from a place of love and surrender rather than striving and pride. That is why it is so easy to slip into religion. The actions on the outside can look the same.

The Bible is very clear in its description of the characteristics and behaviors of a genuine believer. Religion will boil these down to rules and checklists, but the deeper you study Scripture and the more intimately you walk with Christ, the more clearly you begin to see that while actions are important, it's more about the heart. While a religious Christian and a genuine Christ follower may look similar on the outside or on paper, once you get to know them you can tell the difference. A religious Christian operates in pride, judgement, and a (sometimes subtle, sometimes overt) focus on self or self elevation. There is often a feeling of fake-ness about them. The genuine Christ follower operates in love, grace, and authenticity - you can feel the love and freedom they are walking in.

Reflection Questions

Are you truly walking with Christ, making Biblical choices from a place of love and surrender? Or are you checking off the religious rules list? Or, are you overly relying on grace and not even bothering to shift from sinful behaviors (Romans 6:1)?

Do you know on that deep heart level who you are in Christ?

Take some time with the Lord and ask Him to reveal to you what your identity is in Him. Record what He shows you, and really soak in His presence and revelation. Keep the description He gives you handy and read it daily until it is so deeply ingrained that you are walking in your true identity.

My personal journey to freedom from the lies of the enemy and walking in my true identity really started when I began to unravel the lies about God and who I am in Him that I had been taught my whole life. I'll never forget the day in 2017 that it all started.

I was in my early 20's. I had been married for less than a year and was working three part time jobs. I was riddled with stress, fear, anxiety, overwhelm, and depression. It was afternoon, my husband was still at work, and I was sitting in my living room on the couch, watching a live video of this woman who did a weekly virtual bible study. I had listened to some of her videos before and was intrigued by her. Hesitant, because much of what she said did not line up with what I had been taught, but it resonated deep within my soul and so I was intrigued.

On this particular day she was teaching out of 1 John. Specifically, 1 John 4:17 which states ". . . as he [Christ] is, so also are we in this world" (CSB). Her teaching focused on this phrase, and her main point was that we have all the same power and authority right now, here on earth, as Jesus. My mind was blown. Not only had I never heard someone teach this, I had been taught that to consider oneself as equal with Christ in any capacity was absolute heresy and a one way ticket to hell.

But her argument was compelling, and the implications, if true, would be life changing. So I pulled out my Bible, and like my professors at Bible college had drilled into my head, I went and dug into the context of the verse she was using to support her argument. First I read the whole verse. Then the whole chapter. Then the whole book of 1 John. I couldn't find ANYTHING that refuted her conclusion - in fact everything I read proved and supported that what she was saying was true.

As Christ-followers, we have been washed in His blood, and grafted into the tree of the chosen people of God. We are adopted into the family of God, making us co-heirs (read: equals) with Christ in the sight of God. When God looks at us

He sees Christ. And He sends his Holy Spirit to indwell us, sanctifying us, making us more holy and more like Him day after day (if we let him), and as we press into Holy Spirit, He fills us with power and authority - the same power and authority that Jesus has.

I sat there in shock. What? How can this be true? It went against everything I had been taught in the church I grew up in, against everything the Bible college I attended taught, everything my family believed and drilled into me my whole life. But it's there, clear as day in the Bible. And the more I studied, the more the whole of Scripture came alive and pointed to that same conclusion.

With this realization came a massive paradigm shift. I literally could feel things inside me changing. Because this one belief, this one perspective is a foundational element of one's identity as a Christian. Who you believe you are in Christ is foundational to how you walk out your faith. It is the difference between being stuck in a cycle of shame and legalism or being free and empowered.

It also caused me to start questioning everything I had previously believed. Which wasn't too hard, because throughout my whole life there had been a part of me deep down that didn't sit right with much of what was taught and modeled for me. But for the first time in my life I let myself actually explore it. If this is true, what else have I been believing that is not true? If my church, school, and family are wrong about this, what else are they wrong about? The deeper I dug, the more I found the answer to be: most things. Much of the theology and doctrine I was raised under is straight up wrong, and another large chunk has elements of truth but has been twisted and misapplied in order to justify and enable people in leadership roles to maintain control and get away with abuse.

This was the beginning of a massive transformation in my, and by extension my household's, life. Within a few weeks I had joined a coaching program run by the same woman, and I went all in. I devoured every book, teaching, course, and coaching call with a hunger I had rarely known before. All of a sudden things started to make sense, and slowly I began to change. The stress, depression, anxiety, and overwhelm, though not completely gone, began to lift. My walk with the Lord grew deeper, I grew more confident, and overall our life shifted.

That was the beginning, the turning point in my life. There were more times, more moments that had a similar turning point effect, but this was the first, and in many ways the most significant because it was the one that started the shifting and healing of my identity. From there, I continued to pursue healing and take practical steps to shift into and solidify a healthy identity. The most successful of those steps are what I am going to share with you next.

PART FOUR

MAKING THE SHIFT: PRACTICAL STEPS TO CHOOSE AND ANCHOR IN THE TRUTH

Once we know the truth of who we are in Christ, it's our responsibility to believe, accept, receive, and align ourselves with it. Although our old identity is dead, some of the old thought patterns, habits, and temptations remain. God allows these things to remain in order to strengthen and test us (like He did with Israel in Judges 3:1-5). We grow stronger in our faith, conviction, and authority when we are active in the process of releasing the old identity, and each time we resist the temptation to go back, we are proving our mettle in the Spirit. It is our responsibility to choose to resist temptation, change the habits and patterns, and walk in this new identity.

Now, this is not necessarily a salvation issue. We are saved by grace through faith, not by our works. However, Scripture is also abundantly clear that the evidence (proof) of our faith is found in our works, our choices, our behavior, our words, and our actions. There are many passages in the Bible that talk about what a truly Christ-centered life looks like, and dire warnings for those who claim Christ but do not truly follow Him. It is imperative that we do not try to resurrect our old identity. We need to allow it to die and be put off, and then put on our new identity.

In order to do this, the first thing that we need to understand is that this transformation occurs from the inside out. God is not looking for behavior modification, He is looking for heart change. And I can tell you from personal experience not only does behavior modification not work, it actually makes things worse. You need to start on the inside, shifting your beliefs, undoing the tangle of lies, and allowing God to heal your wounds, and then from that inner work, your actions will naturally start aligning.

Let me give you a personal example of one of the ways this is currently (at the time I am writing) practically playing out in my personal life to illustrate this concept: my physical health. I have been at least a bit overweight for my entire adult life, but between 2019 and 2025 between having 4 babies in 5 years and the trauma of one of those babies dying (on top of multiple other stressful things going on) I gained about 90 pounds. At my heaviest in February of 2025 I weighed 325 pounds and was wearing a tight size 24 in jeans.

The crazy thing was, if you looked at my diet and lifestyle, I shouldn't have gained that much weight. Throughout those years as I was gaining weight, I was consistently trying to lose it. I tried multiple diets, eating plans, natural supplements, you name it I probably tried a version of it. The only things I didn't try were surgery or GLP-1s. Nothing worked, it seemed that no matter what I did I gained weight, or in the best case maybe maintained it.

But then, starting in February 2025, just a week or so after my highest weigh-in, I started losing the weight. On the outside this made no sense. We had just moved cross-country on faith, and were living in hotel rooms eating mostly fast food or the cheapest foods we could find because we had depleted our savings and had little to no income. Between stress and diet, I should have been gaining even more weight. But slowly, steadily, it started coming off. What happened?

To answer that we need to look back a bit further. I have been pursuing healing and growth for over a decade, but in the Fall of 2024 I dove deeper into my inner healing than I ever had before. In that season I worked with the Lord (and a Spirit-filled counselor) to break down the amnesia wall that was hiding all those soul-fragments I mentioned earlier and I started to work with them, process the memories, and allow the Lord in to heal and minister to them. By February 2025, most of the soul fragments had reintegrated, and I had a much healthier sense of identity, and a stronger sense of confidence and clarity in my relationship with the Lord and ability to hear His voice, and that inner healing was finally starting to show up visibly in my body.

One of the things that I had worked through was a soul-fragment that held a lot of self hatred, loathing, and self sabotage. Once I worked through that wound and healed and reintegrated that fragment, I stopped hating my body, wishing for it to change, and trying to abuse it into submission through punishing diets and unrealistic goals. I shifted into a place of acknowledging where I am currently, appreciating my body for all it's done and still doing for me, and treating it with genuine love, care, and respect right now. I eat nutritious food in whatever volume feels right at the moment. I move my body regularly, sometimes gently and sometimes pushing it a bit, depending again on what feels good at the moment. I buy from quality brands and wear stylish clothes that fit and are comfortable and look good. I use quality makeup and skincare products. No more waiting until I reach a certain size to invest in clothing and makeup that I like and feel cute in, I get to feel cute and take care of my body well now and in every season between now and when I reach the size that is healthiest for my body.

As I do that and continue to seek the Lord and let Him work in my heart, the weight is letting go and being eliminated from my body. As of the date that I am writing this[12], I have released 30 pounds, and am steadily continuing to release the excess weight without any crazy diets or intense exercise regimens. What has already happened in the spiritual is now showing up in the natural. You see, our bodies often hold onto weight when we don't feel safe or when we have trapped

---

[12] February 6, 2026

emotions or trauma. When we move into a safe place, allow the Lord in to heal the trauma, and process our emotions out in a healthy way, it frees our body to relax and regulate, which often results in excess weight coming off as well.

This is just one example of what the healing and transforming from the inside out rather than behavior modification looks like. It can show up in so many other ways. The key thing to understand here though is that behavior modification does not work in the long run. If you want lasting transformation, you need to start with the inner heart work. But how? Let's get really practical with some steps that you can take right now to take all that you've learned so far and apply it practically to your life in a way that will actually last.

Inner Healing

We're going to start by cutting straight to the deep stuff. Later on I'll also share simple, less intense actions you can do today to start making shifts, but since we're going for heart transformation rather than behavior modification here, I'm going to start where all the changes really start happening: Inner Healing. This is where we dig deep and expose old wounds that are still painful so that we can truly be free. Inner Healing can look like a lot of things, but in my experience there are a couple of key elements: Confession and Repentance, Forgiveness, and Deliverance. The order in which one needs to do these things tends to shift around, sometimes you'll even circle through them a couple of times in one healing session! But these are the core elements to getting full, lasting heart healing and change.

Confession and Repentance

It is hard to mend something if you don't recognize that it is broken, or heal someone who doesn't acknowledge that they are sick. So one key element of inner healing is confession of where we have fallen short. The word "sin" was originally an archery term, and it simply means to miss the mark. In this context, the mark is God's perfection, and sin would be anything short of that. When we fall short, we need to confess (acknowledge where we failed) and repent so that we can receive God's forgiveness and grace to try again.

Both confession and repentance are crucial steps that must happen before we are able to truly move forward in our lives with God. Confession is the part where we acknowledge where we failed to measure up to God's standard. It is the humbling of ourselves before God and positioning ourselves to truly repent. Repentance is when we not only say that we are sorry, but we take actual steps to change and shift. An apology without changed behavior is manipulation, not repentance. True repentance includes a change of behavior. When we have done that, we also need to acknowledge where we are hurting and where we need His help to align our identity properly.

Reflection Questions
What in your life do you need to genuinely confess and repent? Take a moment right now to do that.

Forgiveness

This is a significant, and often mis-taught one. There are a lot of misconceptions about forgiveness in the church. One of the biggest ones is that forgiveness means pretending that nothing happened - even if it is a pattern of behavior on the part of the person who did the harm - which basically means erasing the consequences of the harm for the person who did the harm. For example, say there is a husband who got angry, yelled at his wife, and slammed a door so hard it broke. Eventually he cools off and comes back and apologizes, and she forgives him. Great, except the next day he does the same thing, but maybe this time he broke a dish. Again, he apologizes, again she forgives him. Then it happens again. The third time it happens, she points out that it is a pattern of behavior that needs to be addressed, but his response is, “You said you forgave me, but you must not have actually forgiven me because you are bringing it up again. You are unforgiving and bitter”. This is the type of forgiveness that is rampantly promoted in certain parts of the church, and this false teaching of forgiveness is why abuse is so rampant in those same parts.

False Forgiveness follows a pattern of:

1. Someone hurts or offends you in some way.
2. You address it, ideally in a one on one setting, but occasionally you may need to address it with others present.
3. The person who caused harm says they are sorry.

Occasionally some sort of offer of restitution or attempt to "fix" or "make it up to you" may occur, but you are discouraged from accepting it because a "godly" person will just forgive and say anything more is unnecessary.

4. You say you forgive them, and some sort of reconciliation like a hug or restoration of fellowship time occurs, along with any consequence they should face being greatly reduced or removed.
5. Everyone pretends nothing happened, you are required to grant full access and restoration to the one who caused you harm as proof of your forgiveness, and you are not allowed to talk about the hurt again or you will be accused of being bitter and not truly forgiving.
6. Everyone is happy except for the person who was hurt, but that person is shamed into silence.

This type of forgiveness has been the standard taught in the church, but it is not Biblical, and it actually enables abusers rather than promoting genuine healing and restoration.

So, what is Biblical Forgiveness? First off, you need to understand that forgiveness has nothing to do with the other person. You don't do it for them, and sometimes you don't even talk to them about it. It is between you and God, and it is actually for you. Jesus says in Matthew 6:14-15 that if we don't forgive others, we won't be forgiven, and later in Matthew 7:2 that the standard by which we judge others is the standard by which we ourselves will be judged. Additionally, forgiveness is not a feeling. Forgiveness is a choice. We decide that we will forgive someone, and they don't have to be sorry about what they did or even know that we have forgiven them. It is you deciding what your heart posture is going to be. By forgiving, you surrender your hurts and offenses to God and let Him deal with it.

Now, this does not mean that we have to re-engage in a relationship with the person who did us harm. If they are not repentant, you are allowed to maintain a healthy boundary. Even if they are repentant, you are allowed to require a process and time for trust to be rebuilt (and if they are offended by this, they are not truly repentant by the way). What healthy boundaries look like greatly depends on the relationship, level of harm that was done, and what the Lord is leading you to do. There are some relationships where you are to restore right away, there are others that need a process, and still others where restoration just is not going to happen. There is no one size fits all approach to what restoration looks like, but the key thing here is that forgiveness and restoration are two different things, and they can only be connected by the genuine repentance of the person who did the harm.

I know this goes against what a lot of Christians believe because I was taught the false version of forgiveness that equals immediate restoration and pretending nothing happened and never bringing it up again myself. I have even had multiple people accuse me of not operating in forgiveness because I have had to draw some really strong boundaries that include no longer being in fellowship with certain people in my life due to their lack of genuine repentance.

So let's break down the process of Biblical Forgiveness:

1. Someone hurts or offends you in some way. You have feelings about it. Those feelings are valid and need to be felt and processed - but not wallowed in.

    Note - some people will say that addressing the issue with the person is the first step, and depending on the nature of the relationship it can be, but there are also times when it may not be safe or advisable to address it with the person privately or directly (such as active abuse or legal situations, or when you have already addressed a pattern and they are not repentant). So at some point you may or may not address it with them, depending on the situation. Whenever it is safe and healthy, you should attempt to address it, though I personally recommend walking through forgiveness before even attempting to address it with the person, because as I said earlier, forgiveness is about your heart posture, not the other person. I have found that making sure my heart posture was already in forgiveness makes the times when I need to address something with someone go smoother, regardless of their attitude.

2. You feel those feelings and take them to the Lord. Acknowledge them, tell Him what happened, and get everything you're thinking and feeling about it off your chest.

"Dear Lord, _____ did _____ and it made me feel _____"

3. When you are ready to make the choice, choose to forgive. Again, this is not a feeling. You may still feel hurt. You may still feel angry. But forgiveness is a head choice, not a feelings choice. Tell the Lord who you are forgiving, and what you are forgiving them for. Be as thorough and detailed as you need to be.

"Lord, I choose to forgive _____ for ______ and how it impacted me by _____. [name] I forgive you."

4. Release them from your heart of any obligation to pay you back or make it up to you in any way.

"I release you. You owe me nothing."

5. Bless them to receive conviction and healing from the Lord.

"In Jesus name I bless _____ to receive deeper revelation of Him and to turn to Him in repentance."

6. Ask the Lord to cleanse your heart from any unforgiveness that may want to hold on, and give your feelings to the Lord.

"Lord, I ask that you cleanse my heart and remove any remnants of bitterness or offense over the things that I have forgiven. I give you my feelings and ask that you renew my heart with your perspective on this situation."

7. Amen! Now, you have chosen forgiveness so you do not dwell on it anymore in your heart. If it comes up again, remind yourself that you forgave that, and give it back to God. Sometimes we may need to walk through this process of forgiveness for the same person or even the same event multiple times. If that happens it doesn't mean that you didn't forgive, it simply means there are deeper levels of healing you are walking through.

That is the process of Biblical forgiveness. If the person who harmed you is repentant, then you can go through a process of restoration as led by the Lord. But if they are not, you get with the Lord and ask Him what appropriate boundaries would be in the specific situation. If you are unfamiliar or struggle with boundaries, I highly recommend the book Boundaries by Dr Henry Cloud. He is a Christian psychologist who has a lot of Biblical wisdom on the matter. Also know that as you grow in your identity in Christ, you will be better able to establish and hold healthy boundaries.

Reflection Questions

Who and/or what in your life do you need to forgive?

Take the time to write down everything that comes to mind. Realize that you may even need to forgive yourself for not knowing or doing certain things, or God for not doing things as you felt He ought to. Prayerfully process through this list, make the choice to forgive as you are ready.

Deliverance

This is an area that can get really messy and confusing if you are not careful. There are a lot of ideas out there about the concept of deliverance, some more trustworthy than others. Be very discerning and lean into the Lord for wisdom on who to listen to and seek ministry from. However, demonic oppression, possession, and influence is very real, and much more prevalent than we like to think. Therefore it is a crucial element to address in the healing process.

There is a massive misconception in the church that believers cannot be possessed by demons. But oh boy, is that wrong! Believers can be possessed by demons if one or more of certain conditions are present:

1. Someone can be possessed by a demon before being saved, and that demon will sometimes hang around until it is specifically kicked out.
2. A believer can open doors for demons through living in consistent unrepentant sin. This can give the enemy an invitation to come in and make himself at home.
3. For those who have soul fragments, sometimes those soul fragments are in agreement with the enemy and will open the door for demons to come in.
4. In some cases, there can be bloodline curses or agreements with the enemy that open the door for demons to mess with whoever is in the bloodline whether they are Christians or not until the curses or agreements are specifically nullified.

Some common signs that a person could be possessed include but are not limited to:

1. Sudden changes in mood or behavior, sometimes accompanied by memory loss or amnesia, and sometimes accompanied not remembering what you did in certain moods or states.

2. Intrusive thoughts or voices
3. Compulsive behaviors
4. Consistent nightmares, sexual dreams, or dreams featuring spiders, snakes, scorpions, or other demonic symbols
5. Overall feeling of heaviness, depression, anxiety, or fear that you just can't shake
6. Chronic illnesses
7. Paranormal experiences

I know that sounds intense, scary, maybe even crazy. But not only have I personally experienced the truth of this, I have seen it at work in others too. And it's nothing to be scared of. If you are in Christ, you are on the winning team. There is literally nothing the enemy can do to you. I have had demons try to attack me both verbally and physically through the person they were possessing and all I had to do was command them in the name of Jesus and they had to obey.

Now, that being said, deliverance is not something to undertake lightly or without the proper preparation and backup. Some demonic entities are stronger than others, and some take more work to get out than others. There are some that will go with a simple prayer, there are others that it can take hours of working through with the Holy Spirit to get them out. There are also others who, as Jesus said "only go out by prayer and fasting" (Matthew 17:21). In my personal experience of being delivered, I had some that I was able to deal with just by myself with the Holy Spirit, and then I had some that I needed the help of a prayer team working together to get out. And I have had a similar experience when ministering to others. Some demons I was able to cast out with little to no resistance, others required a team of several Spirit-filled believers to deliver the possessed person.

There are so many details and factors that can go into deliverance that are highly personal, because there can be things that give the enemy a legal right to mess with you, and until those things are dealt with you won't experience full freedom from the attacks. Because of this, I strongly encourage you to find a coach or minister who has experience in inner healing and deliverance to support you in the process. I have found that inner healing and deliverance occurs much faster when supported by someone who is gifted in that area.

This is an area that I personally have rapidly growing experience and authority in, however there are many others whose whole ministries revolve around educating the church in these matters, two of whom in particular have helped me tremendously in my own journey. For understanding how the enemy has and uses legal rights to mess with us, I recommend Robert Henderson's books on the Courts of Heaven. There are also many teachings by him on this topic on Youtube. For deliverance, especially around soul splits and extreme trauma, the books and teachings by Dan Duvall with BRIDE Ministries have been instrumental in my personal journey. Both of those resources combined with working with a coach or minister with experience in the areas you most need support in are the best place to start this deeper level of healing.

Reflection Questions
As you read this section, did you feel an intense fear rise up? That may actually be a sign that you need deliverance because the enemy is afraid of being found out.

Did you feel a sense of curiosity, or just this sense inside of resonating with what was shared? That also may be a sign that your soul knows you need deliverance.

Are you willing to explore inner healing and deliverance as a part of your journey to heal?

If so, I recommend looking for ministries or churches local to you that do inner healing and deliverance. If you cannot find any, I suggest looking into some of the ministries listed at the end of the book.

The Spirit-Body-Soul Connection

As we have already discussed, we are a three-part being. We each have a body, soul, and spirit. When we start the journey to healing our identity, it's important to address all parts of our being. While heart change is more effective than behavior modification, it doesn't mean that we neglect our bodies while we are doing the inner heart work. We also need to not neglect our soul when doing spiritual work, and vice versa. Sometimes one area will need more attention and focus than the others in the healing process, but even then it's important to take care of all aspects of our being.

Simple practices like going for a walk each day or stretching before bed can be a good way to care for your body and help it feel loved and cared for. Doing something you love like a favorite hobby or connecting with a friend can do the same for your soul. And taking the time to be present and really tune into the Lord will feed your spirit. Doing one small thing to care for each aspect of your being each day is an important habit to develop so that you can thrive on all levels. Making sure that you are balancing the deep work with lighter things is also important. Emotion follows motion, so as you are digging deep and doing the inner work, take time occasionally to pause from that and make physical changes as well. It can make such a difference.

Practical Steps for Healing Your Identity From the Inside Out

Now we're going to talk about some of the lighter stuff. These things are physical, tangible steps that you can start taking to shift your identity. There is no right or wrong order for how to take these steps. Some of these steps are easier than others, some take more or less time, some are simpler, and some are harder. Plus where you are currently in your journey and what personality type, preferences, background, etc. you have are all factors in what order these steps should be taken. While there certainly are principles that are universal and processes that work for most people, there really isn't any one-size fits all approach to Spiritual Growth (and anyone who says there is is peddling some form of religion). So read through the following steps and see them for what they are: encouragement and suggestions for how to apply what we've been talking about that I personally have done and seen successful in both myself and others. You are free to try any or none of them, mix and match, and figure out where the Lord is leading you.

Heart Posture

We start with an open heart posture. If you're reading this then I'm assuming that you're likely already in this place, but it never hurts to say it. If we want to transform, heal, and embody our new identity, we have to maintain a heart posture of humble openness. Part of the process of transformation is something called sanctification. This is where the Lord strips away the old identity. Transformation is a life-long process, because the goal is perfection like Christ, and as long as we are here on earth in our mortal bodies we will never quite reach that end. Therefore it is crucial to maintain a heart posture of humility and openness before the Lord throughout our entire lives. This is our main call: to be humble before the Lord. If we can do that, everything else tends to fall into place.

Read Your Bible

This may seem super obvious, but HOW you read your Bible is crucial. You can't know God intimately if you don't read what He has revealed about Himself in His word. But you also can't come to know Him intimately if whenever you do read His word you come at it with preconceived ideas and interpretations from others. While there is definitely a time and a place for studying what others have to say about God, deep diving into commentary, and exploring theology, if you don't have a foundation of personal relationship and intimacy with God, now is not that time. You need to start with the basics. Just you and God. Put the commentaries away, turn off the sermons, even put aside your study Bible and get a basic Bible. Take your basic Bible, a journal, some pens or pencils (I'm partial to a combo of Pilot G-2 07 gel pens, some erasable pens, and a highlighter or two myself), and sit down somewhere quiet. Pray and invite the Holy Spirit to teach you. Ask the Lord to reveal Himself to you and guide you into His secret place. Then, open your Bible and start reading, listening for whispers and nudges from the Lord as you do. Highlight the things that stand out to you. Journal your thoughts, questions, prayers, and the insights the Lord gives you as you read His word.

1 Timothy 3:16 says all Scripture is God-breathed (inspired by God) and is useful for gaining wisdom and knowledge. Hebrews 4:12 says that the word of God is living and active. When we look at these two Scriptures together, we can understand that God's word is the main source of information for how to live a Christ centered life, and that it isn't just some boring old tome. It is a dynamic book that reveals new depths every time you study it. I personally have read the Bible cover to cover more times than I can count in my life (at least 10. Pretty sure more than that, but I haven't been keeping count), and yet every single time I sit to study, something new or relevant for where I am right this minute stands out. There have been times when the Lord highlighted one single verse for me, and then gave me pages and pages of insight and revelation from His heart for me. There are other times where I read a whole book in one sitting and get a big picture concept from the

Lord. All of it is so wonderful though. Spending time with Him is the best use of time there is. This is the power and the beauty of developing your own personal intimate relationship with Him and consistently studying His word.

Connect With Like-Minded Community

There have been multiple studies done showing that you become the average of the five people you spend the most time with. In our day and age, this doesn't have to be in person connections either. I think a better way to say it would be that you become the average of your top five influences or inputs. So this could be a person, but it could be a TV show or movie; it could be a podcast or a certain musician; it can be a book or a Youtube channel; it can be a Facebook Group or influencer on social media. It's the five things you spend the most time engaging with and listening to. This principle is important to understand because we aren't always intentional with what we allow to influence us, and it is through these sneaky back doors that we can unintentionally be feeding our old identity rather than transforming into our new one.

One of the most crucial turning points in my journey was about 9 years ago when I stopped allowing anything that didn't line up with the Truth of who God is and who we are in Christ to influence me. I stopped listening to certain podcasts, I donated a ton of books, I even disconnected from some people on social media. I stopped listening to certain musicians and stopped watching certain TV shows and movies. Eventually, my husband and I even left the church we had both been attending since our youth (for my husband he was born into that church, and we had met and gotten married there. So this was a really big step for both of us).

But I didn't just cut all these things out, I replaced them. I replaced the podcasts, books, and social media connections with like-minded ones. I replaced the entertainment and media with things that were more uplifting and aligned with where I am now. We started attending a different church that better aligned with what the Lord was teaching us. I joined an online community of women who were on a similar journey as I was. Now, over the past nine years as I've grown and seasons have changed the Lord has shifted the exact details of some of these things around. Some connections, influences, and resources are only for a season. But some of them can also be for life, and there are a few specific ministry and people connections that have not changed.

The key point of this is: find like-minded influences. I cannot stress enough the importance of getting connected and plugged into a community of people who are like minded as you are on this journey. We are designed to live life in community, and we need that tribe of people who will cheer us on, call us out, and love us well - and that we can do the same for them. Our lives are not our own now that we are in Christ. They are meant to be poured out as a living offering to Him, and one of the key ways we do that is by living in community and using our gifts for the building up of our fellow believers and expanding the territory of the Kingdom of Heaven here on earth. That can only be done in a community.

Adjust Your Environment

Along the lines of surrounding yourself with a like-minded community, you also need to adjust your environment to reflect the Truth of who you are. This can look like a lot of things. It can look like decluttering and organizing your home and car. It can look like getting rid of physical things tied to your old identity. It can look like you choosing to put up verses, quotes, or images on your walls, mirrors, or desk that remind you of the truth. This is actually one of my favorite hacks for memorizing something - write it down and tape it in a couple places that you know you will see multiple times a day, and then every time you do see, take a minute to actually read it and think about it.

What we tolerate in our surroundings is a reflection of what we're tolerating internally. If we are tolerating chaos, clutter, and disorganization in our home, it means we are tolerating feeling chaotic and disorganized internally as well. And since God is a God of order not chaos, if we are tolerating chaos, we are allowing our old identity a foothold. This is not meant as judgement or to shame - believe me, with three kids I have to fight the monster of chaos myself on a regular basis. But when we establish systems of order and routine, the chaos and the clutter are easy to take care of and move on from rather than ruling our lives. That is an environment that reflects the identity of the child of the King that you are.

The same thing applies for your car and your office or desk or other workspace. The places where you spend the most time should be organized, appropriately comfortable, and appropriately decorated/beautified. Being in a pleasant space makes choosing to walk in our true identity easier, so let's make our homes, cars, and work environments the Embassies for the Kingdom of Heaven that they are!

Watch Your Words

Our words are incredibly powerful. What we speak has a tendency to happen. If we are constantly complaining, we get more to complain about. But when we start speaking gratitude and life and God's Word over situations, we get more to be grateful for and we see God's hand more. There are two principles behind why this is true.

Firstly, there is the natural scientific principle. We all have something called a reticular activating system in our brain. What this system does is it takes all the data from our senses and filters out everything that is not relevant or important for us to notice or take in. This is a crucial system because without it we would go into sensory and information overload! One key thing about this system is that we actually can tell it what to keep and what to ignore by our - you guessed it - words! What we consistently say and think programs the reticular activating system and tells it what to focus on. So even if the Lord massively blesses us, if we are continually complaining, we miss the focus of the blessing and see the negatives the majority of the time.

Secondly, there is a spiritual principle at work here too. When we speak in alignment with God's word and will, we are coming into agreement with Him and partnering with Him in what He wants to do, which tends to speed up the process. The more we speak our true identity, the faster we embody it. Conversely, if we are complaining and speaking negatively, we are hindering God's plan because we are not operating in faith. The more negativity we speak, the longer we are stuck there in that negativity. There are countless Scriptures that support this concept. The Lord tells us over and over in both the Old and New Testament to give thanks and to meditate on His words and works. The One who designed us created the reticular activating system, and so He gives us clear instructions on how to program it. I for one think we should follow them.

One of the best ways to do this is to speak God's promises, as well as what He says about you. Something that I like to do both myself and with my children each morning is speak what God says about me as His child in the Word as a personal "I am" statement. So I take the verse and re-word it to be a personal identity statement. Things like "I can do all things through Christ who gives me strength", "I am full of wisdom and understanding, becoming more and more like Christ each day", or "God does not give me a spirit of fear, but of power, love and a sound mind!" are spoken every day before I drop my kids off at school. The more I speak God's words over myself, the more they sink into my heart, and the more I live in line with them.

This practice is so powerful that I compiled a list of my 10 favorite powerful Scriptural Identity Declarations to share with you:

- I have the righteousness of Christ through my faith in Him (Philippians 3:9)
- I have the same power, authority, and strength as Jesus (1 John 4:17)
- I have the mind of Christ (1 Corinthians 2:16)
- I am forgiven, washed clean, and made whole by the GRACE and LOVE of Jesus (Ephesians 1:7; Romans 4:4)

- I am unoffendable because my sin nature has been crucified with Christ and you cannot offend a dead person (Galatians 2:20; Romans 6:6)
- As Christ is, so am I in this world (1 John 4:17)
- I am full of peace and joy in all circumstances because I know that God works ALL things out for the good of those who love and follow Him. (Romans 8:28)
- Today, I choose to walk in the power of the Holy Spirit, and as I do so I exhibit the fruit of the Spirit (Galatians 5:22)
- I am known for bringing peace, freedom, and joy to all environments I enter (2 Corinthians 3:17)
- No weapon, physical or spiritual, formed against me can succeed because I am protected by God. (Isaiah 54:17)

I hope this helps give you some ideas. Feel free to copy them and use them yourself. However, while using the thoughts that someone else has put together is a great starting point, an even deeper shift occurs when we do this type of work for ourselves. So, I also recommend searching the Scriptures yourself and taking God's descriptions of His people and turning them into personal identity statements for yourself. Doing this trains your reticular activating system to find evidence of your In-Christ Identity, as well as training your brain as a whole to think and behave in line with your True identity. Overall it's a fantastic practical tool for the next step: Renewing Your Mind.

Take Your Thoughts Captive and Renew Your Mind

Welcome to one of my favorite topics, and something that I tend to get on a soapbox about: taking your thoughts captive and renewing your mind. It's actually an instruction for us given in the Bible - 2 Corinthians 5:10 tells us to take captive every thought to make it obedient to Christ, and Romans 12:2 says "Do not be conformed to this age, but be transformed by the renewing of your mind so that you may discern what is the good, pleasing, and perfect will of God." If you've been to church, you've probably heard these verses thrown around, maybe even heard sermons on it, but from what I've seen, usually the church focuses on the *need* to take thoughts captive and renew the mind, not *how* to take thoughts captive and renew the mind.

At least that's been my experience. I grew up in the church and one of my mom's favorite admonishments to me was that I needed to renew my mind. The problem was (and still is in many churches) that this instruction was never followed up with a "how" that made sense, at least to me. Occasionally someone might try to explain by saying "read your Bible" or "pray more" or "memorize Scripture". Show of hands - when you're really wrestling with something, how often are these types of comments actually helpful? I thought so. It's not. And for a highly traumatized child and teen, it really wasn't helpful because I already was doing all those things. So what's the answer?

The answer is found in what I like to call the Thought Formula. The Thought Formula is a process based on a life coaching principle that I like to call the Thought Cycle. This principle teaches that our thoughts lead to our emotions which lead to our actions. So the root of our actions is our thoughts or beliefs, even if those thoughts and beliefs sometimes are subconscious. In order to effect heart change rather than behavior modification, we get to get curious about those thoughts. So we start practicing something called metacognition - basically we think about what we are thinking about. This causes us to become more aware of our thoughts, and when we are aware of our thoughts, we are able to hold them (capture them) and then compare them to Scripture to see if they are aligned with Truth. If they are, great! If not, we renew our minds by getting rid of them and replacing them with a new thought. But how? Enter the Thought Formula.

The Thought Formula is a process that I personally use and that I teach my clients to use to help them create new thought patterns that are in line with their identity in Christ and calling in the Kingdom. Now, a word of caution. You may find that practicing the thought formula works for a while but then you fall back into the same patterns as before and you can't quite seem to make things stick. This is a textbook symptom of needing inner healing and deliverance like we talked about at the beginning of the chapter. The Thought Formula will work to a degree regardless of where you are in your healing journey, but the full transformation will only happen if the inner man/ woman is healed and cleaned up and ready to fully receive and embrace the new thought patterns. That being said, here is the Thought Formula:

<u>Step 1</u>

Take the thought that you have become aware of and ask these questions about it:

- How does this thought make me feel? (Really think about this one and explore how that emotion FEELS in your body - for example you may feel defeated, but how does that feel in your body? Do you feel tired, energetic, sluggish, heavy, light, clear, fuzzy, etc.?)
- When you feel that way, what do you do?
- When you do that, what results do you get?
- Are these results fruit in keeping with my new identity in Christ, or my old identity?

If the fruit is in keeping with your identity in Christ, then you may want to stop there and keep the thought. If it's not, move on to step two.

<u>Step 2</u>

If the fruit of the thought is not in line with who you are in Christ, we hold it up to Scripture.

- Is the thought 100% true
- Does it have all the qualities listed in Philippians 4:8?
- Does this thought honor and glorify the Lord?

If the answer to all is yes, great. It stays. If not, on to step 3

<u>Step 3</u>

Repent of the thought and ask the Lord to show you a new one that is in line with His Truth. Write it down and anytime the old thought comes up, refuse to hold it, and instead grab onto the new one.

If you make it a regular habit to go through this process with situations that don't seem to be in line with your identity in Christ, you will find that the momentum and speed will increase and you'll be shifting faster and faster until it becomes automatic.

These suggestions are by no means exhaustive. There are so many modalities[13] out there for healing, growth, and transformation. However these are the ones that I personally have found to be the most impactful for both myself and my clients. As you work on applying what you have learned in this book, always be checking in with the Holy Spirit. He will guide you to the right steps for your unique calling and journey.

[13] Method, model, process

Conclusion

Thank you so much for taking the time to read this book. I hope you enjoyed reading it as much as I enjoyed writing it. Before we fully end this book, I wanted to share some additional thoughts to support you in your journey. If you have any questions about what has been covered in this book, please reach out to me via my business email: AriseinFaithLLC@gmail.com. I would be more than happy to answer your questions, or suggest resources if that would serve you better.

If anything in this book resonated with you, I want you to know that you can experience the same freedom from shame and fear and chaos, the same connection with God, and the same healing, the same abundant joy and life that I have shared my testimony about. You just need to reach out for it. It's there, ready for you to receive it.

Just as a like-minded community is important, so too are personal, one-on-one relationships. Connecting with key people who know you deeply, who can see your blind spots and live life with you is important. But I'm not talking just about friendships. I'm talking about relationships that help you heal faster. Sometimes that can be in the context of a mutual friendship, but if you are dealing with any of the more intense things that have been mentioned in this book, I highly recommend investing in working with someone who has the experience to support you on that deep level.

This type of support typically requires some level of financial investment on your part, and for good reason. The coaches, ministers, counselors, and/or therapists who are qualified to support someone looking for deep inner healing have invested their time, effort, and money into acquiring and honing the skills they use to support you, not to mention the time and energy they give in supporting you. It is only right that there be some sort of financial exchange. It is also Biblical to pay those who minister to you - Galatians 6:6, Luke 10:7, 1 Corinthians 9:14, and 1 Timothy 5:17-18 are just some of the Scriptures that teach this concept. Beyond that, YOU are worth it. Your healing, your growth, and your transformation is priceless.

I know that the idea of paying someone for support, especially for support in inner healing and identity work, may be hard for some of you to wrap your heads around. I know because I struggled with it too. Hiring a coach for the first time was one of the hardest, scariest things I've ever done. I literally felt nauseous after I hit the "submit payment" button. But you know what? I have never regretted a single penny that I spent on coaches and resources that were intended to help me in my healing journey because even if I didn't get exactly what I expected out of it, I always learned something, and each thing worked together to get me to where I am now.

That being said, there's a balance. Scripture is clear that the Holy Spirit is our counselor, and He will guide us to all Truth as we surrender and walk in obedience. However, God also loves to work through people, so sometimes He will lead us to hiring a coach or mentor who will help us break down the walls and get to healing faster. As Ecclesiastes 4:12 says "if someone overpowers one person, two can resist him. A cord of three strands is not easily broken". I have personally experienced the three-strand effect of myself, a coach, and the Holy Spirit working together to accomplish amazing things. If you are stuck in a cycle of shame, stress, fear, or anything else we have talked about in this book and you can't seem to get out of it by yourself, maybe it's because you're not meant to. Find a mentor. Connect with a community (I have a free one that you can join right now - scan the QR code at the end of the book). Healing comes in relationships.

It's simple, but not easy, to choose healing. But you don't have to walk that path alone. If you're ready to heal but want someone who's gone before and knows the way, reach out. There is a place and a space for you.

Recommended Resources

Coaches

Amanda Stout

Amanda walks Christian men and women ages teen to adult through uncovering what is really holding them back from the life and relationship with the Lord that they desire, and then guides them through the process of breaking down those obstacles so that they can truly enjoy and thrive in their purpose and calling in the Kingdom of God.
You can connect with her via her website:
https://ariseinfaith.app/

Kelsey Murdoch
Kelsey is a certified master coach, boundaries expert, and emotional wellness advocate. She excels in helping her clients heal on a spiritual, emotional, and physical level from various traumas and challenges.
You can connect with her via email: **kelsey@kelseymurdoch.com**

Clair McDaniel

Clair McDaniel is a master life coach and soul integration mentor specializing in trauma informed nervous system regulation, and identity restoration. She guides individuals through deep transformational work to address childhood wounds, reclaim their God breathed identity, and live from clarity and purpose.
You can connect with her via her website: **clairmcdaniel.com**

Shannon Nortz

Shannon is a certified life coach specializing in money mindset as it relates to all aspects of life. She excels at holding safe space for her clients to dig deep into what is causing them to feel stuck in all areas of life.
You can connect with her via email:
movingmountainscoahing@protonmail.com

Books

Forgotten God by Francis Chan

If you are unfamiliar and/or uncomfortable with the reality of the present day presence of the Holy Spirit, I recommend that you start with reading Forgotten God by Francis Chan. He explains in a clear and Biblically grounded way how the Holy Spirit is still alive and active, and how by developing our connection to this person of the Trinity, our relationship with God comes alive.

The Courts of Heaven (series) By Robert Henderson

These books are fantastic resources for inner healing and learning how the Spiritual Realm works so that we can be more effective in our Kingdom assignment.

The Serpent and the Soul by Katie Souza

This is a great resources for specific spiritual warfare if you are feeling like you keep getting stuck in cycles that normal approaches don't seem to help.

Prayers that Shake Heaven and Earth by Dan Duvall

This is a great resource for spiritual warfare whether you are beginner or have experience with inner healing and deliverance.

Organizations/Ministries

Soul Shaker Live Nashville

This ministry specializes in deliverance and inner healing, They do live events in their local area, but also have a podcast and educational social media posts among other resources.

BRIDE Ministries

This ministry specializes in inner healing and deliverance specifically for those who have experienced extreme trauma and Dissociative Identity Disorder.

Sources

Works Cited

Books:

Samuel Chadwick, "Humanity and God," in *Humanity and God* (London: Hodder and Stoughton, 1904), 15–16.

Christian Standard Bible (Nashville, TN: Holman Bible Publishers, 2020),

Websites

Gheorghica, Jonathan. "*What Are the Seven Spirits of God?*" Ffministry.com, 3 Jan. 2023, www.ffministry.com/blog/what-are-the-seven-spirits-of-god

Norma Umphress. "T*he Seven Spirits of God.*" Awakegloriousbride.com, 17 Nov. 2022, awakegloriousbride.com/2022/11/17/the-seven-spirits-of-god/. Accessed 17 Jan. 2026.

Works Consulted

"The Names of God • an Essential List of 200." Chronic Joy®, 2 Sept. 2025, chronic-joy.org/names-of-god/.

"16 Names of God That Reveal His Character." Mission Hills Church, 2021, www.missionhills.org/16-names-of-god-that-reveal-his-character/. Accessed 17 Jan. 2026.

"Names of God – the Good Way." Thegoodway.live, 2024, thegoodway.live/resources/prayer/names-of-god.

About the Author

Amanda Stout is a trauma-aware faith-based life coach, writer, and speaker. She equips and empowers Christians who feel stuck in cycles of shame, pain, and disappointment to A.R.I.S.E. into their Kingdom identity and calling through teaching, resources, 1:1 and group support, and community.

Amanda lives in Middle Tennessee with her husband the three living children. Fueled by coffee, chocolate, and Ethiopian food, when she isn't working, Amanda loves to crochet, read, and spend time with her family and friends.

You can connect with Amanda by visiting her website:
https://ariseinfaith.app/

Or by scanning the QR code below.

www.ingramcontent.com/pod-product-compliance
Lightning Source LLC
LaVergne TN
LVHW010932110826
845149LV00013B/2557

* 9 7 9 8 9 9 4 8 7 5 8 1 0 *